Advance Praise

"Bits of brilliance on golf, and life from individuals associated with game in so many ways, competitor, architect, or in the case of the Hall of Fame writer Dan Jenkins, journalist. The advice, despite the title, is relevant to individuals of all ages. Arnie's in there—'Treat others as you would want to be treated'—Jack, Tiger, Greg, Phil, all the greats.

There's a haunting observation from Errie Ball, who was the last living entrant in the first Masters 'By the time you read all these nice letters,' he wrote to Nick Acquisto. 'I'll be gone.'

Gone also is Jack Fleck, who beat Ben Hogan in the playoff for the 1955 U.S. Open at Olympic Club. 'Be fair and honest to everyone," wrote Fleck. "You will have some ups and downs in life; but get up again and do your best...' Words to remember."

   – Art Spander, *Oakland Tribune* columnist, California Sports
      Writer of the Year

"A collection of incredibly insightful advice for your 'lucky boy' from thoughtful individuals with their priorities square in the crosshairs of life.

May God bless both you and your son, follow the advice offered and the world is his oyster."

   – Steve John, CEO, Monterey Peninsula Foundation

Wisdom for a Young Golfer

Wisdom for a Young Golfer

Collected by
Charles J. Acquisto

Apprentice House
Loyola University Maryland
Baltimore, Maryland

First Edition

Printed in the United States of America

Hardcover ISBN: 978-1-62720-049-3
E-book ISBN: 978-1-62720-050-9

Design by Marianne Magot

Published by Apprentice House

Apprentice House
Loyola University Maryland
4501 N. Charles Street
Baltimore, MD 21210
410.617.5265 • 410.617.2198 (fax)
www.apprenticehouse.com
info@apprenticehouse.com

The First Tee®

In celebrating the game of golf and its life lessons, all of the author's proceeds from this publication will benefit The First Tee, a nonprofit charitable organization dedicated to impacting the live of young people by providing educational programs that build character, instill life-enhancing values and promote healthy choices through the game of golf. The First Tee is a global initiative that shows golf is truly more than a game.

I would like to thank my wife Terri for all her loving support and my three golfing kids, Matt, Nick and Gabrielle, for their inspiration. A big thank you to The First Tee's Jen Weiler and Amanda Robinson for helping make this dream a reality. Finally, a Major thank you to Apprentice House's Kevin Atticks, Valerie Casola and Marianne Magot for believing in this book when so many others took a pass.

Contents

Barney Adams 15

Amy Alcott 17

Peter Alliss 18

John Ashworth 19

Errie Ball 20

Ian Baker-Finch 21

Ricky Barnes 22

Joe Louis Barrow, Jr. 23

Chip Beck 24

Judy Bell 25

Larry Berle 26

Chris Berman 28

Ted Bishop 29

Carolyn F. Bivens 31

Jane Blalock 32

Tommy Bolt 33

Sir Michael Bonallack 34

Jackie Burke, Jr. 36

William Campbell 37

Donna Caponi 39

Billy Casper 40

Bob Charles 41

Don Cherry 42

Tim Conway 43

Alice Cooper 44

Paula Creamer 45

Nathaniel Crosby 46

Luke Donald 48

Dana Dormann 49

Joann Dost 50

Walter W. Driver, Jr. 52

Pete Dye..53

Ernie Els..54

Steve Eubanks 55

Sir Nick Faldo 57

Tom Fazio 60

David Feherty 61

George Fellows 62

Sean Fister 63

Tim Finchem 64

Dow Finsterwald 65

Jack Fleck..66

Marty Fleckman 67

Jim Flick 70

Raymond Floyd..71

Tadd Fujikawa 72

Fred Funk 75

Jim Furyk 76

Kenny G 77

Danny Gans..78

Vinny Giles 79

Hubert Green..81

Natalie Gulbis 82

Coach Jesse Haddock 83

Charles Howell III..84

Walter Iooss, Jr. 85

Juli Inkster 86

Hale Irwin 87

Tony Jacklin 88

Dan Jenkins 89

Peter Jacobsen 91

Don January... 92

Gregory Jones... 93

Mickey Jones 95

Robert Trent Jones, Jr. 96

Cristie Kerr 98

David McLay Kidd 99

Anthony Kim 101

Peggy Kirk Bell... 103

Peter Kostis 104

Matt Kuchar... 105

Trip Kuehne 106

Bernhard Langer... 107

David Leadbetter... 108

Tom Lehman... 111

Justin Leonard.. 113

Brittany Lincicome.. 114

Kenny Loggins 116

Nancy Lopez 117

Davis Love III 118

Butch Lumpkin.. 119

Verne Lundquist.. 122

Sandy Lyle 123

George "Buddy" Marucci, Jr................................. 124

Gary McCord... 125

Mark McCumber 126

Peter McEvoy 127

Jill McGill 128

Jim McLean 131

Steve Melnyk 133

Eddie Merrins 134

Phil Mickelson 135

Steve Mona 136

T.P. Mulrooney 139

Jim Nantz 141

Leroy Neiman 142

Byron Nelson 143

Rick Newell 144

Jack Nicklaus 145

Greg Norman 146

Michael O'Keefe 147

Mark O'Meara 148

Lorena Ochoa 149

Jesse Ortiz 151

Arnold Palmer 153

Dr. Joseph Parent 154

Jerry Pate 156

Suzann Pettersen 158

Gary Player 159

Nick Price 160

Harold Ramis 161

Anna Rawson 162

Beatriz Recari 163

Katherine Roberts 164

Chi Chi Rodriguez 166

Doug Sanders 168

Peter Thomson 169

Alexi "Lexi" Thompon 171

Carol Semple Thompson 172

Patty Sheehan 174

Marilynn Smith 175

Sam Snead 177

Joseph Steranka 178

Louise Suggs 180

Perry Swenson 181

Frank "Sandy" Tatum, Jr. 183

Frank Thomas 185

Kelly Tighlman 186

Bob Toski 188

Lee Trevino 189

Ty Tryon 190

Ken Venturi 191

Peter Ueberroth 192

Bob Vokey 193

Robert von Hagge 194

Dennis Walters 196

Lanny Wadkins 197

Tom Watson 198

D.A. Weibring 199

Tom Weiskopf 200

Michael Whan 201

Jack Whitaker 202

Kathy Whitworth 203

Steve Williams 204

Dr Gary Wiren 205

Tiger Woods 206

Introduction

Imagine walking into a golf course clubhouse to find a proverbial 19th Hole filled with the game's greatest names and personalities. There is Arnold Palmer holding court with Byron Nelson, Sam Snead, Jack Nicklaus, Kathy Whitworth and Tiger Woods. You hear Ken Venturi laughing with Gary McCord, Peter Kostis, Verne Lundquist and David Feherty. Golf inventor, golf yoga instructor, golf comedian, golf trick-shot artist, golf caddy, golf journalists, golf CEOs, golf photographer, and golf celebrities fill out the crowded room. Given the golden opportunity to ask these golf personalities one question, what would it be?

Bookstores and libraries have shelves filled with golf books offering advice on properly hitting a golf ball, working on your short game, anecdotes of what Arnie said to Jack, and what life on the PGA or LPGA Tour constitutes. I have bought and read many of these golf tomes. These books inspired me to try a different approach with people who have become synonymous with the great game of golf.

I wanted to ask these golf gurus and players, many of them a one-person corporation, an all-encompassing question: *How do you define success and set about achieving it?*

Reading varying opinions on how to hit a drive straighter will not make you a better person. However, the answers to the

"Success" questions will not only provide a great path for life, but if applied to golf will help improve your game from the putting green to the 19th Hole.

There is no greater sport than golf for teaching a person, young or old, lessons for life. Integrity, honesty, sportsmanship, and character are the common adjectives associated with golf. While many sports hold to the mantra "You ain't tryin' if you ain't cheatin'"; not golf. A golfer is expected to call penalties on his or herself when most other sports have players either cheating with drugs, bending the playing rules or hoping an official incorrectly awarded a critical play in their favor. Can you imagine a baseball batter calling his line drive down the line foul? Or a football wide receiver popping up to signal he did not catch the pass? How about a basketball player whistling himself for traveling? How about a hockey player voluntarily checking himself into the penalty box?

Knowing golf can teach young and new players to the game a lot about defining one's character, I could find no better place to explore the "Success" question than the best and most famous names the game has to offer.

In addition to the best golfers' advice helping shape future generations, I wanted this book's proceeds to benefit The First Tee, a youth development organization established by the World Golf Foundation in 1997. Since golf is a metaphor for life, The First Tee program teaches life skills to young people ages 6-18 how the "Nine Core Values" displayed on any golf course can transfer to their daily lives. The Nine Core Values are honesty, integrity, sportsmanship, respect, confidence, responsibility, perseverance, courtesy and judgment. These values can be found sprinkled throughout the advice letters contained in this book.

It should be noted this advice collection grew out of my son Nicholas' first birthday present from me. After his June 13, 2001, birth, I began writing famous people asking if they would impart advice to Nicholas on how they define success and how a person can achieve success. Of the dozens of professions I mailed letters, I was amazed at the incredible response rate from one particular group of people: professional golfers.

While a good response rate is one letter received back for every three letters written and mailed, the professional golfer return ratio was ridiculously high. Nearly every famous golfer gladly returned a letter to Nicholas, many of them handwritten as requested.

I do not have an answer as to why golfers were happy to oblige my advice request. I can hazard a guess that the golfer's upbringing, education and the nature of the game instilling strong character skills played a role. Golfers may lead all athletes in being asked by the public for advice, whether it is how to cure a nasty slice off the tee or how to putt with more consistency on the green. Giving advice and asking for advice is second nature to these men and women. Knowing there was much more to learn and to pass along to Nicholas, I decided to explore the best the game of golf had to offer.

In pursuing this quest, I discovered a maxim golf has taught me for life. The more I learn, the less I know. For every Lee Trevino and Gary Player, there was a Bill Campbell and Carol Semple Thompson to be discovered. For every Tiger Woods, there was an Errie Ball. This learning process provoked me to examine all the game of golf had to offer.

My love for golf did not begin until 1982, my freshman year at

St. Vincent Pallotti High School in Laurel, Maryland. During a mandated, one-week spring semester sabbatical, my baseball coach Steve Walker introduced me and a couple dozen Pallotti boys to the golf game as a worthy elective. Prior to that day, the most golf I had watched involved either the television reruns of the Three Stooges or those Little Rascals spraying the ball around the course. With little instruction other than the general direction of the first tee box, my high school golf class was turned loose on Paint Branch Golf Course, a Par 3 track a Tiger Woods drive from the University of Maryland campus.

Now the early 1980's might have been golf's Dark Ages period. The Big Three of Arnold Palmer, Jack Nicklaus and Gary Player were no longer major contenders, leaving the PGA Tour largely nameless. Jokes about golfers 1970's fashion faux pas of tacky TV-test pattern pants with overly colorful shirts dominated stand-up comedians' acts. A tee time could be had at nearly any course on any day at the last minute. A twosome on the hole was far more common than a foursome. Public golf courses were succumbing to developers' bulldozers and planned communities. The most popular golf ball was orange colored. Yes, our golf bags' ball holder looked more like a Crayola crayon box with orange, yellow and Pink Lady golf balls.

Being a left-handed golfer, I had no southpaw pros to emulate and finding lefty clubs was as easy as locating a Victoria's Secret store in Vatican City. A Northwestern starter set was my first golf clubs. I would use these wood and metal sticks for the next 14 years.

From 1982 to 1995, I dabbled in golf. In high school, I worked the bag room at Turf Valley Country Club, earned a paycheck at Rocky Gorge Driving Range and spent many a summer day knocking a golf ball around Allview Golf Course in Columbia, Maryland. Still, the golf bug failed to infect me or much of the country. Allview Golf Course closed. My Loyola College Division I team's head coach courted my roommate Nick Milano and me to play despite our combined handicap of 35. The PGA Tour lacked a dominating American player to help sell the game. Many sports fans used televised golf as a snooze inducer.

After graduating from college, I fell back into the game through my job: sports journalist. Writing for *The Montgomery Sentinel* newspaper, I was privy to covering the PGA Tour's annual stop in Montgomery County as the TPC Avenel hosted The Kemper Open and for two years the Bethesda Country Club was the site of the LPGA Championship. Having interviewed every kind of athlete from high school to professional, I was struck by the professional golfers' engaging personality and willingness to provide answers beyond the cliché sports quote.

How far has golf come in the last few decades? Allview Golf Course is back (renamed Fairway Hills Golf Course), weaving its way through houses. St. Vincent Pallotti High has a golf team. The Loyola College Golf team recruits well enough to make the NCAA Division I tournament. The PGA Tour has had guys named Tiger, Lefty, Bubba and Boo who play on The Golf Channel. My son Nicholas belongs to The First Tee of the Tri-Valley. Finally, I have been hard pressed to find a single orange golf ball on any course or pro shop for quite some time.

Chuck Acquisto
September 2014

From: **Barney Adams**

Golf equipment enterpreneur,
founder of Adams Golf, proponent
of growing the game of golf

Dear Nick,

First, you should be very proud of your Dad for coming up
with a great idea. Second might seem almost contradictory, but
take all these comments as opinions, or even beliefs, but draw
your own conclusions. We (the letter writers) may have some
degree of success in golf, but that does not mean we possess
great wisdom. Our society tends to over-recognize people who
have been fortunate, but most of us are pretty ordinary in most
aspects.

The best advice I can pass on was given to me over 50 years
ago. I was lucky enough to win a scholarship from a company
in Syracuse, NY, near my home. I was happy to get the award
because it came with a summer job and they were very difficult
to come by in those days, especially paying the top rate of $.85
per hour.

My first day on the job, my boss told me something I've never
forgotten. He said, "Young man, you will have many jobs
in your life. Whatever they are, you try to be the best. If it's
sweeping floors, be the best sweeper. I don't care what the job,
you will get satisfaction from being the best you can be."

I never forgot his advice and now pass it on to you. It's a great satisfaction knowing you try to do the best you can, and there is a very practical reason for this approach. Whatever field you choose when it comes to a job, you'll learn that the greatest thing you have to offer is service. Others may have products that are equal, but if you have the habit of working to be the best, you will win the service game which means you'll be successful in business.

Respectfully,
Barney Adams
October 29, 2007

From: **Amy Alcott**

Professional golfer, course designer
and member of the World Golf Hall
of Fame

Dear Nick,

Wishing you all the best in your life's pursuits.

Follow your dreams and passions as my grandmother Anna
would say, "always go with your right foot."

All the best,
Amy Alcott

From: **Peter Alliss**

English professional golfer,
BBC television presenter and
commentator

Dear Nick,

Golf

1. The game is there to be enjoyed, so enjoy!

2. Try your best at all times, this is all you can do. Failure is no disgrace.

3. Try not to be "a pain in the neck" – try to use your common sense all the time.

4. Be a contributor – watch and mark everyone's tee shots and second shots when they go into the rough – it all saves time.

   And perhaps most important of all:

5. Make sure the people behind you are enjoying their game and are not being held up by YOU!

Good luck!

Peter Alliss
January 11, 2008

From: **John Ashworth**

Founder of Ashworth golf-apparel

Dear Nicholas,

Treat everyone equal and with compassion. Smile a lot!! Ask questions – be humble, take risks. Get in the groove of doing random acts of kindness, it will effect the "interconnected" world in a positive way.

"Giving is living and living is giving."

Enjoy every day, every moment.

John Ashworth
June 4, 2008

From: **Errie Ball**

Welsh-American professional golfer
(1910-2014), who competed in
the first Augusta National Golf
Tournament in 1934

Dear Nick,

By the time you're old enough to read all these nice letters, I'll
be long gone. I wish you all the best. Make sure you have a good
education and aim high.

Sincerely,
Errie Ball
November 4, 2007

From: **Ian Baker-Finch**

Australian professional golfer, best known for winning The Open Championship in 1991

Dear Nick,

Enjoy your game, have fun.

Golf is a game for life and teaches you so much about yourself and your playing companions along the way.

Golf is like life itself, the ups and downs, the birdies and bogies, the feeling of toughing-it-out on the difficult days and the exhilaration of winning or holing that impossible putt when it counts.

From ages 8-80, enjoy the journey.

Ian Baker-Finch

From: **Ricky Barnes**

American professional golfer who
currently plays on the PGA Tour,
won the 2002 U.S. Amateur title

Dear Nick,

This is Ricky Barnes and it is great to have you aboard our great
country. Hopefully some time down the road we will be able to
meet one another or maybe even play some golf. I will advise
you to give 100% to whatever it is you do in life and then you
will have no regrets. This has been my motto and I feel this is
why I have been successful so far in life. Best of Luck in the
future and hope to see you soon.

Ricky Barnes

From: **Joe Louis Barrow, Jr.**
Chief Executive Officer, The First Tee

Dear Nicholas,

As you reach your seventh birthday, I encourage you to persevere through life's challenges. Whether you're presented with a difficult homework assignment or a tough bunker shot, face those challenges head on. Even if you struggle in your first attempt, you will gain the knowledge to improve in the future.

My mother always said, "There's no such word in the English language as can't." Those words have inspired me to pursue my dreams and have given me the strength and determination to be successful.

Sincerely,
Joe Louis Barrow, Jr.
May 30, 2008

From: **Chip Beck**

American golfer, four-time winner on the PGA Tour and shot a 59 at the 1991 Las Vegas Invitational

Dear Nick,

One thing for certain, to be successful in any endeavor you must have a vision of what you would like to achieve. This vision will enable you to find a way to get there. Every part of your body will conspire to catapult you to the place you envision. The earlier that you cement this vision in your mind the more your chances are enhanced to achieve that goal you have set.

By following your skills and hear you will find the place that you are most qualified to achieve, which will bring much happiness and a way to change the world. Your most significant contribution will happen by following this path. There is more wisdom in planning for success rather than just hoping it will happen.

Nicholas, be certain that there is always room at the top, and that the world will open its arms to make sure that people accomplish what their heart tells them is possible. You have to look no farther than Nelson Mandela, Winston Churchill, or Ronald Reagan, so keep the faith through perseverance, and hard work and anything is possible.

Most Sincerely,
Chip Beck
March, 2008

From: **Judy Bell**

American amateur golfer, inducted into the World Golf Hall of Fame in 2001

Dear Nick,

Do I have advice for you as a golfer? Yes. And it is the same advice I would give you if you chose to <u>never</u> play golf.

Be honest. It may take a while to catch up with you, but you only hurt yourself if you do otherwise.

Persevere. It's easy to give up. Keep trying and you will amaze yourself and others.

Learn the rules. Everything will be much easier if you understand the pieces that make up the whole.

Have fun. Life and golf can be serious deals but if you have fun you will love both.

I wish you every success in life – both on and off the course!

Judy Bell

From: **Larry Berle**

Author of *A Golfer's Dream*

Dear Nick,

Your dad asked me to write this letter to you, to offer you some advice through golf and life. First of all you are a lucky boy to have a dad who would go to this effort for you. My dad would never have done that, but that is another story.

I spent my working life in the concert promotion business, so I was around many celebrities and musicians. I do have a college degree, but I think that my tenacity and desire to succeed was the biggest factor in helping me in business. I was willing to ask agents, managers and performers to perform concerts in Minneapolis and I got good results.

Your dad found me by reading a book I wrote called *A Golfer's Dream: How a regular Guy conquered the Golf Digest List of America's 100 greatest golf courses.*

He went to the trouble to find me and ask me to write to you. This is the exact same way I got onto these Top 100 courses, many of which are private, most are VERY private. I had to find a member at every club to invite me to be their guest for a round of golf. But I kept asking people I met to help me reach this goal and I found, as your dad is finding, that people love to help other people. My wife even wanted me to title the book, "Just ASK".

So my advice to you is: decide what you want and don't be afraid to go for your dreams and goals and don't be afraid to ask. Good things come to people who ask!!

One more thing; remember what Shivas Irons said in *Golf in the Kingdom*: Golf is a metaphor for life: the things we experience on the golf course are just microcosms of our full life. So use golf as a way to learn to live.

Dream Big and Live Bigger,

In helpfulness,
Larry Berle

P.S. If your dad was Jack Nicklaus, your name would be Nicholas Nicklaus and if you were a saint you would be St. Nicholas Nicklaus, not bad with Christmas rolling around.

From: **Chris Berman**

American sportscaster, ESPN

Dear Nick,

May you go through life with a bounce in your step, a smile on your face, acquire and dispense wisdom from your brain, and above all, have a strong and large heart. You will need them all, but no worries. You are capable of every one of them!

Yours truly,
Chris Berman
June 21, 2005

From: **Ted Bishop**

Co-owner of the Legends Golf Club in Franklin, Indiana, and former PGA of America President

Dear Nick,

In the summer of 1971 I got a job working at the Rolling Hills Par 3 Golf Course in my hometown of Logansport, Indiana. It was just that – a summer job. I had never played golf at that point in my life and little did I know what was in store for me. After my second summer of working at this little par-3 course I decided to change my college major to Agronomy/Turf Management and be a golf course superintendent.

When I graduated from Purdue University my first job was at the Phil Harris Golf Course in Linton, IN. I was hired as the golf course superintendent, but I made my living doing the things that a golf pro would do like renting golf cars and selling merchandise. Eventually, I passed my Playing Ability Test and earned my PGA membership.

It was an unlikely start to my career. Never in my wildest dreams would I have imagined the journey that I would embark on after becoming a PGA member. Ultimately, I went from being involved with the Indiana PGA to becoming the 38th President of the PGA of America, which is the largest working sports organization in the world.

In my time as PGA President, I stood against the USGA's ban

on anchored putting. It was my privilege to name Tom Watson as the Ryder Cup Captain. I handed the Wanamaker Trophies to Jason Dufner and Rory McIlroy. I became an advocate for new and different ways to help grow the game of golf. During my term, the PGA of American and the PGA Tour become great allies helping advance our sport. There were numerous television, radio and print media interviews. I traveled the world following, playing and administrating golf.

I could never have imagined back in the summer of 1971 where golf would take me. From a modest beginning in golf to becoming the President of the PGA of America, my advice is this. Chase your dreams, don't be afraid to take risks and never under estimate your potential!

Sincerely,
Ted Bishop, PGA

From: **Carolyn F. Bivens**

First woman to hold the position of commissioner of the LPGA

Dear Nicholas,

Your Dad wrote to me asking that I share a few words of wisdom for young golfers. I certainly hope you have the chance to participate in golf during your life as it truly is a sport to be enjoyed by all – with family and friends – for years and years. While I didn't start playing until my mid-20s, it is a game I encourage all kids today to start as soon as they can grab a club. Be patient. I quickly learned perfection wasn't required or likely to be achieved in my case; just having the desire and confidence to play was all that was needed. Golf brings together people from all walks of life and with varying skill levels who share a common bond – they all love golf. And, no matter what you do, golf will teach you life skills that will be a great benefit to you for the rest of your life. Best of all, God saved some of the most beautiful vistas in the world for golf courses. Give golf a try.

Sincerely,
Carolyn F. Bivens
February 20, 2008

From: **Jane Blalock**

Retired American professional golfer, winner of 27 LPGA Tour events in all

Dear Nick:

The game of golf has made such a difference in my life. I learned a few very special lessons from the game at a young age. I did not grow up as the daughter of a country club family, in fact, my parents did not even play golf. I played golf because I wanted to, rather than it being forced upon me. I was only told to enjoy the game and have fun playing with my friends.

The incident which has had the greatest impact happened when I was 14 years old; playing the final of the Club Championship, I was 5 holes down with 6 to play and took the match all the way to the 18th before losing. I was rewarded by my parents for not giving up and for walking off the green with a smile on my face!

The moral of the story is that is you give it everything you have and never succumb to a negative thought, you will always come out as a winner.

Kind regards,
Jane Blalock

From: **Tommy Bolt**

American professional golfer, winner
of 1958 U.S. Open and World Golf
Hall of Fame Member

Dear Nick,

When you are older and out in the world – select what you
would like to do – and work hard at it – you will be successful.

Sincerely,
Tommy Bolt

From: **Sir Michael Bonallack**

English amateur golfer, one of the
leading administrators in world
golf and World Golf Hall of Fame
Member

Dear Nick,

I always found that some of my greatest disappointments in golf
led to some of my most memorable experiences.

I believe that this can be so if you can learn from the mistakes
you make and make sure that, if a similar situation occurs, you
do not repeat them.

I can think of a number of rounds in which I have been playing
really well and then made a silly mistake by trying to play
a spectacular shot, when a safe option would have been the
answer.

This happened to me early on in my career before I won my first
championship.

I reached the final of the English Amateur Championship and
was two up and four to play when, with my opponent having
missed the 15th green, I tried to play my second shot directly at
a very difficult pin position, rather than playing for the middle
of the green. As a result, I left myself a very hard chip shot and
took three to get down and lost the hole and the match, as he
not only did get down in two, but it gave him the confidence to
birdie the next two holes.

I did not make that mistake in any of my other finals and went on to win five British Amateur Championships and five English Amateurs.

When I was even younger, I had a trial for the English Boy's team to play Scotland the week before the British Boy's Championship. Although I played well, I was not selected. However, I decided to show the selectors they had made a mistake by not picking me and went on to win the Championship the very next week, beating some of the team in doing so.

In the same way, when I was selected for my first Walker Cup team, the amateur equivalent of the Ryder Cup, the captain did not play me on either day of the two day match against the USA.

Again, I decided to prove him wrong and to try even harder and subsequently played in another eight Walker Cups.

This is where I believe golf can teach us so much about life. There are many times in life when we either do stupid things, or think we have had a raw deal because things have not gone our way. Rather than sit back and feel sorry for ourselves, to use the golfing approach, we just have to try a bit harder and make sure we don't repeat the stupid things.

There are good bounces and bad bounces. Forget the bad ones and be grateful for the good ones.

Good luck,
Michael Bonallack

From: **Jackie Burke, Jr.**

American professional golfer, won the 1956 Masters Tournament and PGA Championship. World Golf Hall of Fame member

Dear Nick,

It's a pleasure to be writing you – I have advice with three words and two numbers – First thing first.

50-50 – if you earn 50 – don't spend 51.

Keep your family together, a strong family is your answer – and something for you to work for – not just yourself – Be good Nick, I will be pulling for you –

Jack Burke
2006

From: **William Campbell**

American amateur golfer, two-time
President of the United States Golf
Association and winner of the 1964
U.S Amateur. World Golf Hall of
Fame Member

Dear Nick,

Your father's kind invitation for me to offer advice to you
inspires the following response – especially since this is New
Year's Day of '08 and I could use such a reminder for my own
edification. You have already received many letters from well-
wishers, so I defer to their collective wisdom and perspective
from their individual vantage points. Accordingly my advice is
"short and sweet," intended for a young fellow whose life lies
mostly ahead thankfully; so make the most of it –

When you look in the mirror, who do you see? – not the
youngster you are, but the man you will become. You have the
wonderful opportunity to make of yourself whatever you wish
if you pursue it with focus and determination. So aim high, in
terms of personal traits and career potential, and don't settle
for less. A large part of your future will be determined by you
integrity and character, as well as your effect on others; be true
to yourself, but don't forget that you live in a world of people, all
with their own problems. Try to avoid life's pitfalls by avoiding
wrong behavior and attitude – thus keeping your eye on the ball,
in order to be in all ways you best self, all the time.

You have my best wishes for a Happy New Year and a good and productive life.

Sincerely,
Bill Campbell
January 1, 2008

From: **Donna Caponi**

American LPGA Tour professional
golfer, member of the World Golf
Hall of Fame since 2001

Dear Nick,

Keep your family close. They are your sounding board and are
always looking out for your best interest. The most successful
athletes have had a strong parent or parents to get you thru life's
ups and downs.

Stay in school, study hard and don't do drugs. You never know if
you have an injury, your career could be over and will need that
education to fall back on, especially with what young people are
going thru today to get a job.

Don't let the fear of failure be greater than your desire to
succeed!

Donna Caponi

From: **Billy Casper**

One of the most prolific tournament winners on the PGA Tour from mid-1950s to mid-1970s, World Golf Hall of Fame Member

Dear Nick,

"Right is right even if no one is doing it."

"Wrong is wrong even if everyone is doing it."

Billy Casper

From: **Bob Charles**

New Zealand professional golfer,
one of the most successful left-
handed golfers and winner of the
1963 Open Championship, World
Golf Hall of Fame Member

Dear Nick,

My advice or wisdom for a young golfer is to consider two
words "respect and discipline". Discipline your lifestyle and have
respect for all people.

Regards,
Bob Charles

From: **Don Cherry**

American singer and professional golfer, known for his 1955 Top 10 hit "Band of Gold"

Dear Nick,

The biggest lesson I learned in life, I will now share with you. The Game isn't over yet! By that, I mean never quit on the gifts and talents you are given in life.

I was blessed with a special talent for singing and playing golf. Many times I thought I cheated each talent by not picking one over the other to become the very best at either singing or golfing. However, picking just one talent would have been cheating all those who enjoyed watching me play golf, sing, or both.

Luckily for me, my talent to play golf and sing are two passions I could do my entire life. I was so blessed to have been able to do both at the highest level on the PGA Tour and great music stages, allowing me to meet so many wonderful people and visit unbelievable places.

Enjoy your talents, work hard with your gifts, share them with others, and you will live a rich life.

All the best to you,
Don Cherry

From: **Tim Conway**

American comedian and actor, famous for his 1987 film *Dorf on Golf*

Dear Nick,

I know that you were born on June 13, 2001 in Walnut Creek, California and that your full name is Nicholas James Acquisto. I also know that your mom and dad love you very much.

There are no guarantees in life for being successful or anything else. But I can tell you that if you love and honor your mom and dad and if you show kindness to those around you, you'll be a success without really trying.

Work hard and laugh as often as you can. I know you'll be a terrific person. You can't miss. Your mom and daddy love you so much.

My very best wishes in all that you do....

Tim Conway
June 18, 2002

From: **Alice Cooper**

American rock singer, songwriter, and musician

Dear Nick,

Trust in the Lord. You may forsake him but He will never forsake you.

As crazy as it may sound the older you get, the smarter your parents get.

Be the person your dog <u>thinks</u> you are.

Your pal
Alice Cooper

POSTMARK

From: **Paula Creamer**

American professional golfer on the U.S.-based LPGA Tour, winner of the 2010 U.S. Women's Open championship

Dear Nick:

If you don't have confidence in yourself, why should anyone else have confidence in you?

Nick, never be afraid to raise the bar.

Good Luck!

Paula Creamer

From: **Nathaniel Crosby**

American golfer, winner of the 1981
U.S. Amateur and youngest son of
Bing Crosby

Dear Nick,

What I could say to you could last weeks so I will give you a
poem that I wrote for the young players at the US Amateur
dinner last month.

I encourage all young players to follow their dreams but be
well rounded and have a defined plan as to what they want
to accomplish and the time that they allow themselves to
accomplish it.

Professional goals may not be as important as the "love of
the game". Please don't mix up a desire to be famous golfer
with having a life of appreciation and gratitude from such a
wonderful game.

Nathaniel Crosby

THE HAVAMEYER TROPHY

The Havameyer Trophy it's more than a myth,
It's had so many moments, but it's hard to sleep with.
I found it too heavy to take to school class,
But found the solution while pumping car gas.
I went back to college and would boast "what great luck"
While the Trophy looked good on the front of my truck.
"Think of the prints" this week's winner will sigh,
Then he'll go contract S.F.C.S.I.

To the winner I warn, critics may say it's a fluke,
"On AUGUSTA'S 1ST tee surely he'll puke".
For the young players:
You have all the talent there's nothing you lack,
You're destined to be the next Tiger or Jack.
You're the scholarship kid, the campus hotshot,
From your winning ways you're the best of the lot.
But I ask you to pause and search for your soul,
Because your still in a kind of tiny fish bowl.
What are your goals? You must be exact,
It's just with yourself that you make the pact.
What is it to make it, one win or twenty?
If it's money you seek than how much is plenty?
At the end of the day it's only you, who must care,
To set the right standards it's your own do or dare.
I too was a hit, an amateur hero,
But I turned out to be a professional zero.
In the eighties I saw my success running wild,
So for professional failure I am a true poster child.
So please I implore you to chart out your course,
Where you follow your dreams but don't have remorse.
If your goals are elusive, just limit you time,
Don't be playing at forty on your last quarter or dime.
For those who don't make it, your days still look bright,
So long as you don't prolong a bad fight.
You'll find a new trade, life won't treat you too rude,
You'll make lots of money as the scratch golfing dude.
For the next group of hero's there is nothing to teach,
You'll accomplish those things well beyond others reach.
One day in the future you'll tap Tiger's shoulder and say,
"You played really well back in your day".
You'll speak up and shout, "I will take Tiger down"
You'll be anxious to say, "I'm the new kid in town".

From: **Luke Donald**

English professional golfer, World
Number One in 2011

Dear Nick,

My parents always taught me to treat people how you would
like to be treated yourself. Success is hard to measure, but I have
always been a firm believer in the Law of Attraction. If you want
to be successful, you have to see it in your mind and believe it
has already happened, and the universe will find a way to grant
your wish.

All my best,
Luke Donald

From: **Dana Dormann**

American professional golfer, played
on the LPGA Tour

Dear Nick,

I am happy to pass along some of what I have learned in my first
40 years.

     1. Hard work always pays off. It may not pay off today
or tomorrow or this year, but the satisfaction of knowing
you have put your best effort forward will give you a sense of
accomplishment and contentment.

     2. I believe in the Golden Rule. Do onto others as you
would want done to you. Karma has a way of catching up with
you.

     3. Be kind and respect your family. If you do, no matter
how high you go or how low, they will always be there for you.

Sincerely,
Dana Dormann
November 25, 2007

P.S. My son is one week younger than you and we live close by.
Maybe we'll see you on a golf course or sports field some day.

From: **Joann Dost**

Golf landscape photographer,
former LPGA player

Dear Nicholas,

What compels me and I find valuable about golf is that there are
many aspects of the game which can be interpreted and applied
as life tools or lessons.

Golf requires much of its players. It requires practice. So do
most thinks in life in order to do them well. If someone makes
something look easy, it is most likely due to the amount of
practice they have invested. Golf teaches humility, as even
when we practice until we are completely spent, technique and
consistency often elude us. It is at these times that we must take
a deep breath and be humble. Humor also helps at these times.
Golf is (most often) a quiet game. In these days of immediacy,
golf slows us down and allows us to get quiet. It encourages us
to focus on the present moment, and seems to reward us when
we do so. Much of this is due to the fact that the game is played
in the setting of Mother Nature, so it fosters an appreciation for
the outdoors and for the elements; golf connects us with our
environment. The game is also about acceptance, yet coupled by
strategy. Again, this parallels life. We must accept "where" we are
and strategize on the next "shot". As we accept and strategize,
it helps if we are open to the support and insight of friends and
mentors. In this way, the game promotes camaraderie. Players
share the ups and the downs with their foursome. Golf equally

is based on a player's accountability for his or her actions; good shots and bad shot, good moods and rotten moods. As a result, how you handles what transpires during a round of golf is very telling about your personality. Throughout the course of a round, other aspects of life are touched on from presenting yourself well; dressing respectably and following dress codes for golf courses and clubs to abiding by the rules including handicaps that are established to foster friendly competition and being courteous to your fellow players with a hand shake regardless of whether you win or lose. You must be punctual; if you are late for a tee time, you can be penalized or even disqualified. And when you complete your round, your honesty and integrity are vital as you attest to your own score. From the time you tee off to signing your score card when you've completed your round, there are valuable lessons in golf.

The rules and rituals of playing the game are in place to be respected and incorporated into what has become known at the golf lifestyle. This lifestyle exists on and off the course. More than a life "style", for me the fundamentals have become a way of life. They represent a way of being in the world that is, above all, respectful. The game and industry surrounding the game have afforded me tremendous opportunities and both personally and professionally and for this, I am appreciative and recognize an importance and core value of golf. Hopefully you will experience some of the best aspects of the game and will carry them with you and share them with future generations.

Sincerely,
Joann Dost

From: **Walter W. Driver, Jr.**

Former USGA President

Dear Nick,

I am honored to provide a few thoughts for *Wisdom For a Young Golfer.*

People who achieve to their maximum potential, in every field, lead more robust, interesting and stimulating lives because they usually get to associate with other accomplished individuals. This exposure and stimulation, in turn, produces more potential and opportunities.

This principle applies absolutely in golf. If one is perceived as trying his best, respecting the traditions, sportsmanship and values of the game, other golfers will take him into their friendship and often try to provide opportunities (in golf and other fields) for him. On the other hand, boorish behavior, lack of respect for all elements of the game, etc. can produce doors that are closed to him and limit the endless opportunities available to those who love the game, honor and abide by its spirit, and hand it down to the next generation, just as your father is doing for you.

Yours very truly,
Walter W. Driver, Jr.
March 7, 2008

From: **Pete Dye**

Golf course designer

Nicholas,

You have certainly received great letters from some very distinguished people.

I have been very fortunate to be in golf. You will find fine people in golf. Best in Golf to you.

Pete Dye
March 3, 2007

From: **Ernie Els**

South African professional golfer,
former World No. 1 and winner of
four Major Championships

Dear Nick,

To me, the most important role we play in life is that of a parent. We get one chance in life to be a good parent – make the most of it.

Ernie Els

From: **Steve Eubanks**

New York Times bestselling author
and award-winning writer

Dear Nick,

As a golfer who has been fortunate enough to play the game
on every continent except Antarctica with people ranging from
plumbers to presidents, carpenters to kings, I know first hand
that golf presents an opportunity to see places, meet people, and
do things that no other sport provides. Golf is a great equalizer.
No matter what you do for a living; no matter who your parents
are, or where you live, or where you go to school, you are no
different than the person standing next to you on the first tee,
whether he is the chairman of the world's largest company, or
a truck driver out for a quick round. You are both golfers. And
there's nothing better than that.

As the father of sons, I have told my boys that they are neither
above nor below any man. They came into this world as naked,
crying babies, and will someday leave it like everyone else.
During their brief visit on this planet, they should treat everyone
in life the way they would treat a stranger on the golf course.
If they do that, they will walk a much smoother path through
life. The same is true for you, Nick. Treat everyone as a golf
partner and you will have more than enough friends to carry
you through all your days. If you cherish those friendships -- the
people you meet, and the experiences you share – you won't have
to worry about that new job or that promotion, because you will

have discovered riches that very few men ever find.

Best of luck to you, and I hope this tidbit of advice serves you well.

Steve Eubanks

From: **Sir Nick Faldo**

English professional golfer on the
European Tour, on-air golf analyst,
six-time Major Championship
winner and World Golf Hall of Fame
Member

Dear Nick,

When I first became a professional golfer, I was 19 years old and I'd spent every moment that I could on the golf course for three or four years before that. Since then, I've spent more than thirty years in the business of golf and, whilst I'm not sure whether that qualifies me to give anyone advice on life, I'd hope that it puts me in a good position to pass on a thing or two about life on the golf course.

I've always felt that the most important thing in golf – in any sport actually – is self-belief; truly knowing that you can do something gives you the power to go and do it. It's hard to pinpoint exactly what it is that gives the best players that sense of self-belief, but they've all got it. When I was playing professionally though, I used to focus on three things:

The first was 'preparation'. The more you know about something, the more you feel comfortable with it. If you're driving a car and you don't know what's round the bend, then you're always going to hold back. But if you know what's coming, then you can zip round every corner. When you're prepared for any eventuality then it's always full steam ahead.

Secondly, there was technique; learning about your swing and how that performs, giving yourself the tools to actually go out and do it. Practice, in this case, might not make you perfect – but it will definitely make you a whole lot better than before!

Finally, you need to put all that into action – how do you pull the trigger, give yourself the ability to stand up and do it? It's the difference between being on the range and standing on the first tee at a tournament. I used to practice so much that I had total belief in my golf swing, but then I had to put it to the test under pressure and that's completely different – that's where you need to control your emotions and give yourself the belief.

When you work on all of these things – when you feel fully prepared, when you trust in your technique and know that you can put those things into action – then I used to feel that I could truly believe in my game. I always used to think of it like a neat little circle that just keeps feeding off itself. Confidence in one of these areas gives you confidence in the next and so on, all the way to the 18th hole.

Another thing that I think is very important in golf is visualization. On the golf course, it's no good getting an image in your head of the last bad round you played or the ball heading off into the trees. But if you keep seeing the ball going down the fairway, onto the green and into the hole then you're set up for a great round. Tiger has a great line to describe this - recently he said: 'I putt the ball into the picture.' Here's a man that's seen hundreds of thousands of putts sink – create that picture and visualize that ball going into the hole. It really helps you to believe that you can do it, to do anything in fact.

Finally though, I'd say that you've got to have passion. If you love something, then you don't count the hours. It should never be a case of 'I've got to get in two hours practice' - whatever it is you're doing in life, if you're passionate enough about it, then you'll want to be at it all day. I made it a goal to give it everything until I was 45… I didn't want to get there and think that I could have done more. Now I can look back knowing that I never wasted a moment in my golfing career.

Of course, it should also be about having fun along the way. So don't dwell on the bad ones, focus on the next shot in hand – the one that you can actually control. Agonizing over every mistake is just going to spoil what should be a perfectly enjoyable round of golf.

In fact, that might be just about the best advice that I can give about golf or anything else:

Enjoy yourself out there.

Happy golfing,
Nick Faldo

From: **Tom Fazio**

Golf course architect

Dear Nicholas,

As you go through life, I would encourage you to devote the time and energy to endeavors bigger than yourself. Not endeavors which will bring you material gain or earthly notoriety, but endeavors which impact the lives of others and leverage whatever skills, knowledge and opportunities you have been given. Any achievements I have personally attained in my career cannot compare to the joy I have experienced over the year seeing positive impacts on the lives of others. Strive to make a difference for generations to come. Make that your legacy.

Sincerely,
Tom Fazio
June 15, 2014

From: **David Feherty**

Former professional golfer on the
European Tour and PGA Tour, writer
and broadcaster with CBS Sports
and Golf Channel

Dear Nick:

Be very nice to your little sister, as one day she will have friends in whom you will be very interested. Remember, they will probably trust her advice. Never tie your shoelaces in a revolving door, or wipe your arse with the label off a broken beer bottle — it may be holding onto a shard of glass. Scream at the top of your voice until your parents buy you a beagle — they are hard work to start off with, but you will never have a better friend. Carry a clipboard and walk quickly, it will get you anywhere. And finally, if your heart is arguing with your head, it means they are both distracted, and you can really do what you want!

been there - did that!

best,

[signature]

From: **George Fellows**

President and CEO of Callaway Golf
Company from 2005-2011

Dear Nick,

I'm going to share with you everything I know about golf.

1. Manners matter. Be courteous to everyone. All the time.

2. Honor and fair play are imperative (as is replacing divots).

3. Practice, diligence and hard work pay off.

4. It helps if you dress well.

5. Be bold, take chances, but be careful.

Interestingly, what I know about golf also applies to life. What a game!

Best,
George

From: **Sean Fister**

World Long Drive Champion 1995, 2001, 2005

Dear Nick,

Surround yourself with positive people throughout your life and listen to their advice. Know that you can do anything you can imagine, you must be eager to earn your lot in life by having a work ethic that can allow you to achieve the results that you see in your mind.

As you mature you will realize that family is what you always come back to no matter where you go in life. Keep your family close and involved in your life.

No one will believe in you more than your family and no one will be there for you when you need help quicker or longer than your family.

Be a dreamer and dream big. If your mind can see it it can be. I hope that you have a life full of achievement and love.

Sean "The Beast" Fister

From: **Tim Finchem**
Commissioner of PGA Tour

Dear Nick,

Based on your father's request for this letter, I can only surmise that he recognizes golf as a truly special sport, appreciating not only its challenges and joys, but also the values and life lessons it embodies that can help you in your personal growth.

Whether or not golf ultimately becomes a sport for you over the long term is your own decision. A parent can only help introduce and provide the opportunity to play. The rest is up to you.

Golf is a lifetime sport, and it never stops teaching us about ourselves. All golfers learn that the game's principles can help in school, at home and how they interact with others. It can do the same for you, Nick.

Yes, golf is a wonderful sport. It is fun, challenging and rewarding. But when you embrace the spirit of the game, it can mean so much more. You don't have to become a star to appreciate the impact it can have on your life.

Sincerely,
Tim Finchem
November 16, 2007

From: **Dow Finsterwald**

American professional golfer, winner
of 1958 PGA Championship

Nicholas,

Remember; "Advice not sought is seldom welcome." Since your father asked me to do this, here goes.

Try to do the right thing because it is the right thing, not because of any reward other than your knowing you have done the right thing.

And conversely avoid doing the wrong thing not because of punishment you might receive but because you know deep down it is wrong.

Good luck young man.

Sincerely,
Dow Finsterwald
January, 2008

From: **Jack Fleck**

1955 U.S. Open Golf champion

Dear Nick,

Love your father and mother, as they love you. Lister to your parents, you will be wiser by it.

Learn to love school, as your will use your education all of your life.

Be fair and honest to everyone.

You will have some up and downs in life; but, get up again and do your best, as it will always come out all right.

Enjoy the simple things in life; the sun, trees, flowers, birds, daylight, night, rain, fresh air and all the beautiful people you meet.

Keep this in the back of your mind every day, "As You Think, So Shall You Be!"

Take care of you body, by eating and drinking only the things that are good for you!

Enjoy every day, keep smiling and may God Bless You Always.

Jack Fleck

P.S. Be sure to take up golf, it's the Charm of Life!

From: **Marty Fleckman**

American professional golfer, played
on the PGA Tour in the 1960s and
1970s, 1965 NCAA Champion

Dear Nick,

My name is Marty Fleckman and I would like to share my
journey with you as to where I've been and where I am not. Golf
has been great to me and had a tremendous influence in all the
decisions I have made in life.

My parents were very supportive and gave me the opportunity
to exploit my golfing ability. I was fortunate to attend the
University of Houston on a golf scholarship where I was a
member of three NCAA National Championship Teams (1964,
1965 and 1966). I also won the 1965 NCAA Individual Title.
These accomplishments were very exciting and gratifying to me
especially because Byron Nelson had been my golf instructor
beginning in 1964, and by his help I was able to take my talent
to a winning level.

After graduating from college I made the 1967 Walker Cup
Team and led the U.S. Open at Baltusrol as an amateur
going into the final round. Of course Jack Nicklaus won the
tournament. I then attended the 1967 PGA Tour Qualifying
School and won my first PGA Tour event after acquiring my
playing status. I was on top of the mountain and life could not
have been better. Everything I had ever dreamed of was coming
to fruition. I continued to play well and made the top 60 money

winners in 1968 but stated playing poorly in 1969, even though I competed in The Masters that year. I eventually lost my exempt status.

Most people think that playing golf for a living is the greatest thing on earth. It's like any other profession, when you are doing well it is enjoyable, fun and exciting. However, when you're not, your life is full of frustration, depression and disillusionment. At this point you get into a state of self-pity, you blame others (it's always someone else's fault) or you always have an excuse as to why you failed. Either way you're in a complete state of denial. We are all products of our won decisions because the decisions we make determine the life we live.

My frustration continued in 1973 and I was competing in the Sahara Invitations in Las Vegas. I was so confused with my golf game that I could not function physically and was a nervous wreck. I had completely lost sight of who I was and felt as through I was in a room by myself with all four walls were closing in on me. So the night before the first round of the tournament I contacted the PGA Official and withdrew from the tournament. It turned into being the most important decision in my life because through a friend I went to see a golf teacher by name of Carl Lohren. It was because of Carl that I accepted Jesus Christ as my personal savor and entered God's Plan forever, and that was something for a boy who was raised under Judaism from Port Arthur, Texas.

Believing that Jesus Christ died on the cross as a substitute for my sins completely changed my priorities in life. You see Nick, it is not what you do in life – it is what you think that really matters. It was no longer who and what I am but who and what

Jesus Christ is. It goes to show that everything in life happens for a reason, and this was God's way of telling me that He had other plans for me.; those plans did not include being successful on the PGA Tour because I eventually left the tour. God gave me something better; I have a wife of my dream, the house of my dreams and the job of my dreams as the Director of Instruction at BlackHorse Golf Club in Houston, Texas. I received the 2007 Southern Texas PGA Teach of the Year Award and have been inducted into the University of Houston Hall of Honor, along with a host of other honors.

We all experience some sort of adversity in our lives. Adversity is in evitable and stress is optional. Adversity is what others do to you and stress is what you do to yourself. Everyday you go to the golf course is a test of your capacity for life because that are so many variables and outside distractions that affect your score. In life Nick, there are so many outside influences that can get you off course. Keep your priorities straight and stand for something because if you stand for nothing, you will fall for anything.

Your friend,
Marty Fleckman

From: **Jim Flick**
Golf instructor

Dear Nick,

Your dad asked me to provide some advice for you to achieve your full potential and to have a full and happy life. Here are my guidelines to live by:

These are some guidelines observed from very successful people I have observed in my life's experiences

1. Understand and have no fear of failure as it is part of the learning process. But eliminate those failures going forward.

2. Make sure you have passion for whatever field of work you decide to make your occupation.

3. Learn to handle your disappoints, because your attitude will determine your level of success more than your talent.

Jim Flick

From: **Raymond Floyd**

American professional golfer,
member of the World Golf Hall of
Fame since 1989

Dear Nicholas,

I would encourage you to take up the game of Golf. Golf is truly a game of a lifetime. It is played outdoors in beautiful surroundings, where one gets to encounter nature at its very best. It is a gentleman's game played with sportsmanship and integrity, which builds character and respect.

If one leads their life by the rules of the game of Golf, they will likely grow up to be successful and a true credit to society.

Sincerely,
Raymond Floyd
February 2, 2008

From: **Tadd Fujikawa**

Japanese American professional golfer, youngest golfer ever to qualify for the U.S. Open

Dear Nicholas,

I was very happy when your dad asked me to write you some words of advice. I looked at the impressive list of people that had already written to you and wondered what advice I could give you beyond their letters that might be helpful. I decided that I would give you the same advice that has been shared with me and that I have always chosen to follow. Don't ever give up and don't ever let someone tell you that you are not capable of doing something.

I was born on January 8, 1991, three and a half months premature. I weighed 1 lb. 15 oz. Doctors advised my parents that I had a 50-50 chance of living and being normal. After one week, I had to go through several surgeries and then more when I was about six months. My grandfather later told me that when I was born, he could hold me in the palm of his hand.

After surviving my first year, I went onto lead a fairly normal life as a kid. I was always small, but found ways to use it to my advantage. From the ages of 8-12, I was a four-time national judo champion. My family always taught me to do my best, never give up and always believe that I could succeed. I never thought there were things I couldn't do.

I began playing golf for fun when I was 8. However, I didn't focus on golf until around 11. I really enjoyed it because it was very different from judo. In 2006, when I was 15 years old, I became the youngest person in history to qualify for the U.S. Open Golf Championship. People could not believe it because I was so young and because I was only 5'1" tall. However, I did not see either one of these things as a negative. A few months later, I became the second youngest person to make a cut in a PGA Tournament, the 2007 Sony Open in my hometown of Honolulu, HI. That weekend was one of the most exciting times of my life. All of the fans, and even the PGA Tour players, were rooting for me to do well. It was an amazing experience. I remember doing an interview with Nick Faldo who is a famous golfer. Because he was tall and I was not, I stood on an ice cooler for the interview.

I made a very controversial decision later that summer when I decided to become a professional golfer at the age of 16. This was very uncommon and not a very popular decision at the time. This was a very difficult decision for my parents. However, it has definitely given me the opportunity to grow and get proper instruction from a top PGA teaching pro.

I am now 18 years old. Since turning professional, I have been able to travel around the world, meet many great people and play some of the greatest golf courses in the world. I am now living my dream. I know I have much to learn and many things I can improve on. However, I know this would not have happened for me without the proper support of my family and friends and the lessons I've learned from the things that were supposed to be "disadvantages" to me. If I would have allowed people to make me believe that I was not big enough, strong enough or fast enough, I would not be living my dream or writing this letter to you.

My advice to you Nicholas is to never let anyone tell you that you CAN'T do something and never give up on your dreams. If you work hard and do your best, you will find a way to succeed in anything you really want to. Also, treat people with RESPECT no matter what age, race or sex. If you do these things, I believe you will be a great success and a very happy person.

I wish you all the best in whatever you choose to do.

Mahalo,
Tadd

From: **Fred Funk**

American professional golfer, plays on the PGA Tour and Champions Tour

Dear Nick,

Many times in life you will be told what you cannot or will not achieve. You will be told that your goals are too high, you are not good enough, you will never make it. There are the people that never make it or never try. "Never Say Never!" Having tried even in failure usually leads to learning and satisfaction. Don't be one that says "What If," be one that says "I gave it my all."

All the Best,
Fred Funk

From: **Jim Furyk**

American professional golfer, FedEx Cup champion and PGA Tour Player of the Year in 2010

Dear Nick,

First of all, success is difficult to measure. Only you will be able to measure your own success. I fully believe you have to love what you do to be successful at it. Therefore, choose something you love, set your goals high, work hard, and always believe in yourself! Remember – you only have to make yourself happy to be successful!

Lots of Luck,
Jim Furyk

From: **Kenny G**

American adult contemporary and smooth jazz saxophonist, played on his high school golf team and won a share of 2001 Pebble Beach Pro-Am title

Dear Nick,

I wanted to tell you why I think golf is such a cool thing to do. In your life, you will have a lot of things that will take up your time and focus. That is a good thing, especially if you find something that you are passionate about (which I hope you will!!). The great thing about golf is that is allows you to take a break from all the never ending details that are happening in your life. It teaches you to just focus on one thing. When you play golf, having focus is the only real way to do it. Just think about the shot that you are about to hit and nothing else. Doing this slows everything down and can give you a much needed break from the things that normally take up your mind and energy, Then, when you return to your "real life," you will have a refreshing new perspective. Think of golf as a "mini-vacation".

I wish you the best in the years ahead and I hope that you find the same passions for life as I did with music.

Kenny G

From: **Danny Gans**

American singer, comedian and
vocal impressionist

Dear Nick,

Start each day thanking God for all the good things in your
life. Then expect something wonderful to happen that day. Be
a positive light in a world of darkness and inspire all who meet
you to also shine their light.

Go get 'em!

Danny Gans

From: **Vinny Giles**

American amateur golfer, winner of
the U.S. Amateur and the British
Amateur

Dear Nick,

It is always encouraging to learn about a young man with a keen
passion to achieve the top level not only in golf, but in life. The
game of golf is in many ways like the game of life. Hard work,
attention to detail, the ability to take the bitter with the sweet,
the willingness to accept failure as one strives for success – all of
these factors apply. Moreover, in golf as in life, you will encounter
people of all types, attitudes, morals and characteristics. Some you
will embrace, some you will avoid, some will embrace, some you
will avoid, some will become your closest friends and others will
be lifelong adversaries. Your ability to deal effectively with each
group may be pivotal to your success.

I'm sure that it has been or will be pointed out to you that golf
is an extremely difficult game to master. In a word, golf is <u>hard</u>.
To reach golf's highest level one must work very diligently. Hard
work does not assure success, but without a great work ethic
you will never conquer the beast. There are many intangibles
that can't be taught but may be achieved. For many years, I have
said "give me a golfer with a great heart, great nerve and real
"guts" and I will take him every day over a more talented player
who lacks those traits." Learn to love the game, learn to respect
the game, its history and its tradition. Read the many available
books on the people who have influenced the game – from

Bobby Jones, Arnold Palmer, Jack Nicklaus and Tiger Woods to the rules makers and administrators. Learn to compete. Never give the game the satisfaction of thinking it has gotten the best of you. Enjoy the highs and accept the lows. There will be an abundance of both. No player, including Hogan, Nicklaus, or Woods has totally mastered the game. If they had, they would probably have walked away. Hogan said as much.

For years and years one of the biggest things in your favor is youth. You will become bigger, stronger and, if you work hard, better. Practice, hard work, practice and desire will take you a long way. Compete whenever possible. Learn to play "with a pencil in your hand." Play by the rules. Play with and learn from players better than yourself. From them you can see firsthand what aspects of your game need improvement. Practice your short game, including the putting, more than anyone else. You will find that is fun, creates touch and imagination and leads to low scores. Who has the most incredible short game in golf today? Tiger Woods! How did he develop it? Practice, Practice and Practice.

Finally, learn to love and respect the game! Whether you take your game to the PGA Tour or not, golf will open countless doors for you. It can be one of your strongest allies and one of your defining assets throughout your life. Friendships, business relationships, lessons in life – they all have a foundation in golf. Seize the game and all its goodness. The very best to you in life and in golf.

Sincerely,
Vinny Giles

From: **Hubert Green**

Former American professional
golfer, winner of 23 professional golf
tournaments on the PGA Tour and
Champions Tour

Dear Nicholas,

The best advice on life I can give to you is to do the best you
can all the time. If you do a sloppy project then you reflect that
you are sloppy If you dig a hold, dig a hole you can be proud of
(bad grammer). If you use improper English it shows a lack of
education. Pride favors not any social-economic background.

Have pride, be proud.

Hubert Green

Dear Nick,

The best piece of advice I have ever received is from my father
John Gulbis. My father and I are very close. For 24 years he has
been my Dad, my friend, my biggest supporter and advisor.
When I was a junior player aspiring to be a professional golfer he
gifted to me a 10-foot banner with a quote and hung the banner
in my room. I read the quote many times a day and worked hard
to apply it daily.

The quote said "success: You can't direct the wind, but you can
adjust your sails." I have used this in golf and life. When I won
my first LPGA event in 2007, my father brought the banner and
re-presented it to me. I think of the quote daily...Good luck
to everyone out there who is striving to achieve their goals and
dreams.

Sincerely,
Natalie Gulbis

From: **Coach Jesse Haddock**

Former Golf Coach of Wake Forest University, who guided team to three NCAA titles (1974, 1975, 1986)

Dear Nick,

You are forming your philosophy, which is your book, under the guidance of your parents – So Do the Right Thing!

Everything that feels good or tastes good is not necessarily the right thing.

There are more positive things you will do in your years, hopefully, many years.

Best Wishes to you, Nick, and your family.

Jesse Haddock

P.S. Enclosed is a brochure of my last year coaching.

From: **Charles Howell III**

American professional golfer, won
the 2000 NCAA title

Dear Nick,

Always follow your dream, and do what you believe in! Don't let
anyone discourage you from your goals.

Charles Howell III

From: **Walter Iooss, Jr.**

American photographer, best
known for his award-winning
images in Golf Digest and Sports
Illustrated for more than 50 years

Dear Nick,

"For every human who has ever loved there shines a star."
-Arthur C. Clark

Walter Iooss, Jr.

From: **Juli Inkster**

American professional golfer,who
won three times on the LPGA Tour
and is a World Golf Hall of Fame
Member

Dear Nick,

Keep your head down and hit them close to the hole – All the
best.

Juli Inkster

From: **Hale Irwin**

American professional golfer, one
of the world's leading golfers from
the mid-1970s to mid-1980s and a
World Golf Hall of Fame Member

Dear Nick,

Remember to respect your parents, study & work hard, and the
good things in life do not come easily.

Hale Irwin

From: **Tony Jacklin**

English golfer, most successful British player of his generation who won the 1969 British Open and the 1970 U.S. Open

Dear Nick,

As a young man I didn't have the benefit of television or video to learn golf. I am self taught. When I became a teenager I came across a poem (the original copy is in the Hall of Fame) it goes as follows:

> *If you think you are beaten, you are*
> *If you think you dare not, you don't*
> *If you'd like to win, but you think you can't*
> *It is almost cert you won't*
> *If you think you'll lost, you've lost*
> *For out in the world you'll find,*
> *Success begins in a fellows will.*
> *It's all in a state of mind.*
> *Think big and your deeds will grow,*
> *Think small and you'll fall behind.*
> *Think that you can and you will.*
> *It's all in a state of mind.*
> *Life's battles don't always go*
> *to the stronger or faster man,*
> *but sooner or later, the man who wins*
> *is the man who thinks he can.*

On the golf course, apart from sound fundamentals, this was my bible. Good luck with it.

Kind regards,
Tony Jacklin

From: **Dan Jenkins**

Sportswriter/author, World Golf Hall of Fame Member

Dear Nick,

First, if you want to lead a happy life, get interested in an honest pleasure---sports, whatever---and don't get impatient with it. Stay with it. Work at it. Enjoy it.

Never take a job you hate. Take a job doing something you like, even if you have to start at the bottom.

Hard work will pay off.

Never take a stock tip from a rich guy. Rich guys don't want anybody else to get rich.

Never join a club where half the guys lisp.

Don't go to Harvard unless you want to become a communist or a socialist.

Sit around a coffee cafe and you can find out what those things are.

Pretend to like football even if you don't. Same with golf.

Soccer is for foreigners.

Relish competition in all things.

You can't appreciate the real joy of winning if you've never suffered loss.

If it sounds like writing, don't read it.

Finally, stick with old-fashioned cheeseburgers. Shoot the chef who tries to put quail eggs and avocados on cheeseburgers.

I have spoke.

Dan Jenkins

From: **Peter Jacobsen**

American professional golfer and
commentator on the Golf Channel

Dear Nick,

Get a copy of Michael Murphy's *Golf in the Kingdom* and read
it front to back. Even if you never hit one golf shot in your life,
this is a powerful tool to help you understand yourself and those
around you.

As it says in the book, if you can enjoy the time in between
your golf shots, then you've figured it out. Life is like a round of
golf – going from one adventure to another. The score isn't the
point…it's the journey getting there.

May God bless you and your family…and I really do hope you
play golf.

Fairways and greens,
Peter Jacobsen

From: **Don January**

American retired professional golfer, winner of the 1967 PGA Championship

Dear Nick,

Golf is a funny game. It was invented for people to enjoy themselves while competing against a course with eighteen different holes. Always be happy with what score you shoot, but never be satisfied. Your score is directly related to how much time you have spent on it.

This is just like life; you get out of it what you put into it.

Have a good time playing golf and remember, it's just a game.

Golfingly,
Don January

From: **Gregory Jones**

Broadway actor, writer and director
of play *Men with Clubs*

Dear Nick,

You are growing up in a time when computers are everywhere,
even the golf course. (In my day, we didn't read our yardage off
a G.P.S. in the golf cart; we looked for a sprinkler head or the
distinctive "one-fifty bush.") So I'm going to put my advice to
you in the language of the digital age – know when to delete the
program.

In golf and in life, you can drive yourself nutso dwelling on a
mistake or a stroke of bad luck. If you made a mistake, do your
best to understand why it happened and how you can avoid
making the same mistake again. If you catch a bad break, find
a way to laugh about it. Then delete the program. Move on.
Don't worry about it.

This rebooting of your mind's hard drive will save you many
strokes on the course and many hours of heartache in life.
When you dwell on a bad situation, you can tend to take your
eye off the ball, neglect what you're doing right now. That causes
you to make another mistake. Then you're REALLY steamed
because you made two mistakes, and as a result you make
ANOTHER one. So, my computer savvy young friend, keep
your "random access memory" from getting bogged down in the
glitches of the past.

When you look back on a round of golf or on a year of life, keep those pesky bad times in the trash folder and remember to replay the good shots and good times over and over.

Good Luck,
Gregory Jones

From: **Mickey Jones**

American musician and actor, writer/singer of "Double Bogey Blues"

Dear Nick,

One day this letter will truly mean something to you.

I am living proof that you can do or be anything you want to be. We all have to work for a living. Focus and find a job that you love enough to do for free.

If you can put out the time, effort and work it takes to work in your field of choice, you will never work a day in your life.

When I am working, I can't wait to get to work in the morning. You can do the same.

I wish you the very best and God Bless!
Mickey Jones
April 23, 2007

From: **Robert Trent Jones, Jr.**

Golf course architect

Dear Nick,

I remember when my dad held my head still and told me not to move it when I tried to hit the ball. He taught me to keep my head still when I swing at the ball – yet golf is not a stationary sport. The skill and passion for golf once gained in youth will travel with you wherever you go throughout your entire life.

Golf is a simple game invented by shepherds watching their sheep five hundred years ago. They were bored, so they used the crooks to hit a wooden ball across the sandy dunes land, called "links" in Scotland, a far off flag marking the hole.

So the land and the course is your opponent, not the friends you are playing with. It is the shape of the land that will challenge you in your game. Of course, you can have a match with them, too, if you wish.

When you are a child, you can play with friends your own age and also with your grandparents. When you grow up you can play with your spouse, if you marry. It is a lifelong game to be enjoyed with friends and family of all ages.

Because golf is an individual sport and rarely played in team competition, golf travels with you throughout your life. Golf courses of all kinds await you wherever you go. I have designed them for you on six continents of the earth. I hope you can play a few of them.

Golf will never let you down. Hit the ball, go find it and hit it again until you putt it in the last hold of the course you play.

Yours in Golf,
Robert Trent Jones, Jr.
August 11, 2014

From: **Cristie Kerr**

American professional golfer who plays on the LPGA Tour, 16 wins on the LPGA Tour including two major championships

Dear Nick,

Never quit.

When I was 10 years old, I was playing in a golf tournament. I wasn't playing well and it got to a point where I know I could not win and I stopped trying. I stopped giving it my best. When I got home I had a long talk with my mother who note pleased with the way I handled myself. That day I wrote a contract to myself and signed it…promising that no matter what, I would never give up and I would never stop trying my best.

I still have that contract.

Whether in golf or in life, you will always encounter obstacles, and I learned that day that you will never reach your full potential if you don't give everything you have.

Best of luck,
Cristie Kerr
August 26, 2014

From: **David McLay Kidd**

Golf course designer

Dear Nicholas,

1. Play nice, and play fair.

2. Obey the rules. Even when others don't, you will know you did.

3. Walk, don't ride.

4. Play the ball where it lies. You will achieve greater satisfaction from extracting yourself from a pickle than taking an advantage you did not earn.

5. Wash your balls.

6. Remove your cap when shaking hands with your playing partners after the round.

7. Use sunscreen.

8. Anyone can play well on a sunny day; how you perform when conditions get tough is a true measure.

9. Do not make or take a bet that you cannot afford to lose.

10. Do not skimp on cheap shoes.

11. Aim high—unless you find yourself in the woods, in which case take your lumps and soldier on.

12. Have three good jokes always at the ready.

13. Make your way to Scotland.

14. Until you can beat Tiger routinely, there will always be someone better than you.

15. Study your competitors; you might learn something.

16. Hydrate.

17. If it is predictable, it is preventable.

18. Make a habit of replacing divots and fixing ball marks. If we all left the earth nicer than we found it the world would be a better place.

Cheers,
David McLay Kidd

From: **Anthony Kim**

American professional golfer

Dear Nick,

It seems like just yesterday when I was in your shoes, and there have been many people along the way who offered me advice that helped me get to where I am today. Over the years I've always been amazed at how many parallels there are between golf and life, so the advice I offer here is meant to help you in both.

Most importantly, love the game and have fun. In one round of golf, you'll likely experience nearly every emotion know to man – happiness when you hit that perfect drive down the middle; disappointment (or frustration and anger) when your next shot finds the water; pride when you execute a shot perfectly that you've been practiving for weeks; and maybe a touch of feat when you're staring at that difficult tee shot on the 18th tee in a close match. Enjoy feeling all of those emotions on the golf course and it will help you as you experience them in life too.

Always give your best. There are going to be days when no matter what you do, it will feel like the tame or the golf course has you beat, but if you know that you've given your best effort then you can walk off the 18th green with a smile on your face.

Believe in yourself. Just like in life, preparation and practice in golf will go a long way towards being successful, but through it

101

all, believing in yourself and your abilities is the key. There will be times in both golf and life that self doubt will creep in, but I was always taught that staying confident in your abilities and your plan will eventually help you win.

Respect. Golf is a game that was built on respect and it is important to show it for your opponent, for the golf course, and for the game itself. The camaraderie in the game, even as you stare down a putt trying to beat our opponent, is what makes the game special. Keep that alive in golf and life.

I have always realized how lucky I am to be in a position to play golf. It's a game where the thrills are the same whether you are playing it professionally, or just with friends on the weekend. Keep that passion for the game alive and it will reward you for a lifetime.

Have fun, Nick!
Anthony Kim
August 4, 2010

From: **Peggy Kirk Bell**

Former PGA Professional, first woman elected to World Golf Teachers Hall of Fame

Dear Nick,

By now I'm sure that you're loving the great game of golf!

I think it's wonderful your dad loves the game and want you to love it also.

I have three grown children and eight grandchildren who love all sports, but golf is their favorite.

I've seen young golfers come to our Youth Camps thru the years and some have gone on to tour. It's a thrill for me at 86 to see the progress golf especially for our youth. Through golf I've been able to go around the world, meet three presidents and serve on many different boards. The opportunities have been wonderful for me and for my family. I have been truly blessed.

Best wishes for all that life has to offer. Work hard and your life-long benefits will be many.

Sincerely,
Peggy Kirk Bell
January 9, 2008

From: **Peter Kostis**

American television golf analyst and instructor

Dear Nick,

     1. Golf is life. To be your best at golf, you must be your best in life!

     2. Make your word impeccable.

     3. Replace judgment with gratitude.

     4. Live in the "now" because that becomes your past and molds your future.

     5. Surround yourself with positive and caring people because golf can be very negative!

And finally…play by the rules and HAVE FUN!

Good luck –
Peter Kostis

P.S. Good lessons never hurt!

From: **Matt Kuchar**

American professional golfer, plays
on the PGA Tour and 1997 U.S.
Amateur winner

Dear Nick,

Follow your dreams!

Matt Kuchar

From: **Trip Kuehne**

American amateur golfer, 2007 U.S. Mid-Amateur champion

Dear Nick,

The harder you work the luckier you get! If you work hard, you will never have any regrets. As Ben Hogan would say, "The secret is in the dirt."

My three rules for life are pretty simple:

1. Tell the Truth

2. Go to class/work

3. Show up on time

Master these three rules and you will have a head start!

Trip Kuehne

From: **Bernhard Langer**

German professional golfer, two-time Masters champion

Dear Nick,

1. By following and obeying God, being disciplined, hard working and determined
2. To love God with all you heart, soul and mind and to love your neighbor as yourself.
3. Love is = to give without expecting anything in return.
4. Happiness is = To Know that God loves you and gave his son Jesus Christ to die for your sins. To know that God made each and everyone of us very special and unique. To have family and friends, with whom we can shar our ups and downs, happy times and sad times, good and bad times with.

May God bless you and give you a glimpse of his Glory. I will pray for you and that you would honor and glorify our Lord and Savior, Jesus Christ, with you life.

Sincerely,
Bernhard Langer

From: **David Leadbetter**

Leading golf instructor

Dear Nick,

I thought I would write to you to see if I could impart a few words of wisdom to a young golfer.

I have spent my adult life trying to help golfers of all levels to play this great game a little better. This resulted in good players becoming great players, average players becoming good players and poor players and beginners just becoming avid golfers. You know what they all have in common Nick? It is the desire to improve and see how far they could go. You see, you never really know what you can achieve in life or golf unless you give it your all and strive to do your very best.

The amazing thing about golfers Nick; is that you can look deep into their souls just by watching them play. Do they try their hardest, or do they give up? Do they have a positive outlook, or are they negative and bring everybody around them down? Do they stay calm, or do they get angry? Do they accept that they are responsible for their poor shots and bad scores, or do they make excuses and pass the blame? Do they realize that some days everything goes great and other days are just the opposite? Do they respect the rules, or do they break them whenever possible? You see Nick; these and many other traits that we see in golf—

we see in life. Golf exposes our weaknesses and our strengths. That is why it is such a great game… golf parallels life!

So, my advice to you is this: Learn to love and respect the game, be passionate and determined, learn about the games history, learn its fundamentals, adhere to the etiquette of the game, cherish your clubs—they will serve you well, enjoy your time practicing and playing, set goals, appreciate and take pleasure in playing with good or bad players, keep expecting the best—even when things are going badly. Aspire to be the best that you can be, no matter whether that leads you to playing on the Tour, going to college and playing golf, being on your high school team—or just simply beating your dad! And, most importantly, do it with honesty, integrity, humility, perseverance and a great attitude—all the qualities that the world's best golfers and truly successful people have in common. Above all else, keep a smile on your face and have fun… and remember; it's just a game—not life or death.

Remember how lucky and privileged we all are just to get to play this game. In a world of turmoil and strife, a golf course is just as it was a hundred years ago—a magical place, a landscape of great beauty where you are close to nature… a place where dreams are realized and lifelong friendships are made. For a period of time, all problems and issues simply melt away as you focus your attention on getting that little white ball into the hole!

Nick, my wish for you is that you have a life long love affair with golf, and that what you learn from the game you apply to your walk through life. If you can do that, you will have a truly memorable journey.

Yours in golf,
David Leadbetter

From: **Tom Lehman**

American professional golfer, 1996
British Open champion and former
World Number One golfer

Dear Nick,

There is a lot that I could write to you about, and much of it would
be interesting, but I don't know how much is truly useful. I have
never been one to feel the need to gain a whole wealth of knowledge
that will never be needed and never be applied. What I have always
enjoyed is learning something that can make a difference in my life,
something that inspires me to want to be a better person, a better
golfer, or just better at something than I was before. Since that is
what I like, that is what I am going to give to you. It is not going to
be a comprehensive bunch of thoughts, but a few highlights.

Maybe the most important thing I could say is to be concerned
about your character and not so much your image. Your image is
who people think you are: your character is who you know you
really are. Only one person truly knows who you are on the inside
and that is you. Live your life and work at your passions in such a
way that there are no regrets, so that you can look at yourself in the
mirror and know that you can be proud of the person looking back
at you. Living your life with integrity will make both the triumphs
and disappointments worthwhile.

It is very easy to take the big things seriously and treat the small
things like they don't matter. Well, I can tell you without question
that the small things do matter. Doing the small things well leads to
doing the bigger things well. Ignoring the details, blowing off the

seemingly insignificant things, leads to failure in more important matters later. Every tournament counts. Every practice day counts. Every putt you hit on the putting green and every shot on the range counts. Do it all with intent, with purpose, knowing that the more you put into the small things and the things that seem to matter least will lead to the ability to perform your best when your best is needed.

Finally, there are two foundational cornerstones that you need if you are to be your best at anything. Without them, there is no way that you can become the best you can be. This is not just about golf, but about everything you do. First of all, you need to love what you do. The reason is this, and it leads directly to cornerstone number two: if you love it, you will be willing to pour your heart and soul into it and work as hard as it as you possibly can. You will never, ever be your best without a passion for what you do and a willingness to do whatever necessary to be your best. You can never have the willingness to do whatever it takes without the passion. Without the passion you will not work as hard at it as someone who has it. You can have all of the talent in the world, but without a love for it, you will lose to a less talented person who loves it more and works harder more often than not. Love for what you do and hard work are the foundational cornerstones to success.

My very best to you, young golfer. Whoever you are and wherever you live, I look forward to reading about you and hearing about you in the future.

God be with you.
Your friend,
Tom Lehman

From: **Justin Leonard**

American professional golfer, 1994
NCAA and 1997 British Open
champion

Dear Nick,

Keep it in the short grass!

Justin Leonard

From: **Brittany Lincicome**

American professional golfer, plays on the LPGA Tour and won her first Major at the 2009 Kraft Nabisco Championship

Dear Nick,

It seems funny that I have been asked to put together some thoughts about wisdom for success for a young golfer since I am only 24 years old myself. Life experience usually produces wisdom and I just have not lived as long as many wise folks. I don't always feel wise, but I do believe that I learn everyday and am eager to gain more wisdom. With that in mind, here are a couple of my thoughts.

Always keep in mind what is important. Family, health, friendships, loyalty and honesty are just a few of the things that I place importance upon. I love playing golf for a living, but golf is my job so I always want to keep that in perspective and know that I am fortunate to have other things that are more important to me. If I have a bad round or a bad hole, I remind myself that there are people that love me no matter what. I have more important things to focus my energy on than a silly mistake or bad day.

Remember where you came from. My parents have always worked hard to provide for me and my brothers. The hard work that my mom and dad demonstrated all of their lives gives me a different perspective. I am appreciative of what I have been given and do not want to lose sight of where I came from. I try to be kind to those around me and know that no one person is more important than another.

Please remember to have some balance in life. I really enjoy life by going to sporting events and concerts, fishing, hanging out with friends, and playing sports. Golf is not my entire life. I am able to get away from the office, so to speak, and enjoy other things (although my office is a pretty cool place to go). I have seen too many of my fellow competitors burn out and not enjoy what they are doing and I think if they were to have a better balance, it might have been avoided.

I have to give you at least one tip for the golf course. Focus on the shot on hand. Do not worry about a bad shot that already happened. You will end up paying a second penalty if you cannot clear your mind of a past mistake. Learn from your mistake and move on.

Thanks for listening to this young pup and I hope to gain a lot more wisdom as I continue to work hard and learn from those around me. Remember how lucky we all are to be young golfers.

Brittany Lincicome

From: **Kenny Loggins**

American singer/songwriter and
guitarist who wrote *Caddyshack*
theme song

Dear Nick,

When you get older, you will understand these words. As it says
in *Caddyshack*, "Listen to your heart!"

God bless,
Kenny

From: **Nancy Lopez**

American professional golfer and
World Golf Hall of Fame Member
with 48 WPGA Tour wins

Dear Nick:

Welcome to the world. Life can
be as wonderful as you make it.
Set your goals high. You can reach them
all. Be Happy and smile everyday.

Your friend

Nancy Lopez
4/5/02

From: **Davis Love III**

American professional golfer,
won 20 events on the PGA Tour,
including one major championship

Dear Nick,

I admire your Dad for looking after your future so well. My Dad
was my best friend, and gave me lots of advice, but the best was,

Follow Your Dream,

And Enjoy the Trip!

I was "trip" growing up so it was advice and a play on my
nickname!

All The Best,
Davis Love

From: **Butch Lumpkin**

Golf and Tennis professional, born
with "short arms"

Dear Nick,

Golf is an incredibly challenging game and a lot of fun to
play. I grew up learning from my Dad and we had a lot of fun
competing with each other as I was growing up. Then it became
something we did as a family and later on a game I played with
my friends. It takes a lot of dedication, practice persistence and a
positive attitude. When I first started we adjusted the golf course
making a par 2 a par 5, par 4 a 5 and a par 5 a 7 adjusting
distances so that I could compete with my Dad. It too me three
strokes to get to a par 2 and 2 to put it in giving it everything
I've got. By the time I was thirteen my best score was 130. As an
adult my best score has been 75.

The great news now is there is a program by First Tee that adjusts
the distances and the holes according to your ability and age.
Wish I had this when I was growing up. Please take advantage
of the opportunity to meet kids and challenge yourself to be the
best...or simply to have the most fun you can.

In talking for First Tee, I have met some great kids and made
some great friends. This is what it is about – enjoying the sport
with friends in a fun competitive environment. To have more
fun and raise your level of play I would like to share with you
the TOP Principles. The T is for trust. You must trust that you

have ability and dedicate yourself to giving your best. You must also learn to trust our instructors and the other people there to help you. The O is for organize. You must first organize yourself by getting the right clubs that fit your body and your ability. So get the right clubs. Next find the right books on golf. Go to the public library. There are plenty of books you can read. Get books that have freeze-frame pictures you can look at and learn from. When I wanted to be a tennis professional, I check out every book on tennis so I could se a perfect body and learn the fundamentals. Organize your time for practice because this is what make syou better and increases your confidence. The P is for persistence. No matter what don't let anyone tell you that you can't do it. When they say "you can't", you smile, erase the "t", now you have an "I can" attitude, which will take you a long way.

I have been an accomplished Tennis Professional and enjoyed doing the impossible my whole life. Everyone said it couldn't be done. But I had the belief and faith that I could. Now I am enjoying a golf career playing and putting on golf exhibitions with a 6-inch driver. I would never have believed that as a child. Growing up I could only hit a golf ball 120 yards with a driver. Now I average 260 or 270 dead straight. I have even won a long drive contest at Furman University in a tournament and achieve a hole in one and played in a Nationwide Tour event. All of my friends are professional athletes and hit the ball 300 yards or more. I can't. What I do is hit the ball dead straight, while my opponents ny hit it farther, they aren't always in the fairway I know my clubs and their distances very well; therefore giving me a good short game. Putting is also a great place to make up for strokes. If I have a fad hold, I take my punishment and the hole is over. I make up for it on the next few holes.

A sense of humor is a must in playing golf. One day playing a par 5, a friend of mine almost drive the green, hitting his drive over 500 yards, and then hit on in two and three putted achieving 5. It took me three strokes to get on and I 2 putted achieving a 5. I commented, "If I had your arms I would have attempted the green." The scorecard didn't know how long he drive, only that we both had a 4. Don't focus on what you don't have, but one what you do have. Attitude will take you a long way.

Last piece of advice, share your abilities and gifts with others in the sport, because this is when you realize what you know and increases your confidence. Put God in your golf and make it about honoring the gifts he has given you and in helping others. Use golf to help raise money for charities and learn to embrace the TOP principles and one day I will be watching you on TV and asking for your autograph. "The impossible is just an opinion shared by those who never try. Possible is a word shared by those who think I can."

Wishing you the best in golf and life.

Sincerely,
Butch Lumpkin

From: **Verne Lundquist**
American sportscaster, CBS Sports

Dear Nick,

When you awake each morning, try to see the day that is in front of you as filled with all kinds of opportunities and delights. When you go to bed each evening, think a little bit about what pleased you, what disappointed you, and how you might have approached situations and circumstances in a slightly difference way.

As you grow older, follow your heart. Be your own man. Don't be afraid to step outside the box. Don't be afraid to shatter some glass.

Treat everyone with kindness. Don't let hate enter your heart.

It's a big, wide world out there. Explore it. Expose yourself to other cultures. Be amazed at the mosaic of life. Allow for art and music and dance to be a part of who you are and who you will become.

Above all, stand tall.

All the best.
Verne Lundquist

From: **Sandy Lyle**

Scottish professional golfer, winner
of two Major championships

Dear Nick,

My Father was a club pro. I take many of his wisdom from him.
Watson and Gary's advice are priceless. My Father always said,
when I was fourteen going to tournaments "I have my spies
watching you." At 52, still haven't found them yet.

Best Wishes,
Sandy Lyle

From: **George "Buddy" Marucci, Jr.**

U.S. Senior Amateur winner in
2008, Walker Cup player and
captain

Dear Nick,

Success is not easy. Hard work, honesty and determination
are keys. Most of all treat people the way you would like to be
treated. Keep a smile on your face and a passion for what you
love inside. Follow your dreams, always!

All the best,
Buddy Marucci

From: **Gary McCord**

American professional golfer,
commentator, author and actor

Dear Nick,

Walk through life on paths with no traffic and concentrate on making mistakes, they are the Yoda to learning.

Also, it doesn't hurt to have a sizeable trust fund.

Gary McCord

From: **Mark McCumber**

American professional golfer, played
on the PGA Tour and Champions
Tour

Dear Nick,

Always make it your goal to treat everyone with respect. Treat
them exactly the way you want to be treated.

Show special honor to your Mother and Father. Believe in
yourself. Once you think something is worth doing, do it to the
best of your ability.

Confidence along with humility will make life enjoyable for you
and those around you.

All the best!
Mark McCumber

From: **Peter McEvoy**

British amateur golfer, golf course designer, golf administrator and golf writer

Dear Nick,

You are going to get lots of advice from pro golfers and you should really pay attention to it because these are experienced people and high achievers.

I am going to give you some advice from a slightly different perspective, that of an amateur golfer.

I have seen so many young men pursue a dream of turning pro and who have dedicated their whole life to this one aim. My advice is not to give up on this dream or any other dream you might have but to pursue it with an eye on what happens if it doesn't work out!

In almost all cases the best form of back up is education. With education you can always change direction if your first choice dream turns out to be unachievable.

There is no shame in having this back up, quite the opposite. I know hundreds of young inspirational golfers who wish they had continued their studies and not just put in the work on the range.

"Oh, and keep your head down!"

Kind regards
Peter McEvoy

From: **Jill McGill**

American professional golfer on the
LPGA Tour

Dear Nick,

One of the best experiences I've ever had on the golf course was
playing with Johnny Unitas in the Kraft Nabisco Pro-Am. I
knew of Johnny through all the great stories I had heard. I knew
he was an awesome athlete and one of a kind. I was thrilled for
the opportunity to experience his greatness for 5 hours.

The first thing that struck me was on the first tee, the first shot
of the day. Johnny had a condition which hindered the function
in his left hand. He had rigged a golf glove with Velcro that
secured his left hand to the club. I was amazed that somebody
who had lost enough strength in his hand he couldn't hold
on to the club would still have enough passion to play golf.
Not just the driver required the wrapping of the Velcro; every
shot required the extra help. When I asked Johnny about his
condition and whether it hurt or not his response was "not
enough to keep from me doing something I love".

Every week on tour we play in Pro-Ams. Ninety-nine percent
of the amateurs are great company. Every pro has experienced
the "overly excited", or "highly competitive", or "I wish I had
ear plugs" sort of guy....you get it. These partners are very rare
and my MO is to try to kill with kindness. On this particular
day playing with Johnny U we had a humdinger playing partner!

Our partner was more then willing to offer unlimited and unsolicited advice to everybody in the group. For the sake of this story, let's just call him Ed. Ed was quick to let my partners and I know exactly where we could improve with our putts, reads, chips, club selection……again you get it. I'm trying to paint the picture for you. It is very difficult to push me over the edge during a Pro-Am, but on this particular day I was about to jump off the cliff.

Ed was really enjoying enlightening Johnny with his knowledge of the golf swing and his thoughts on how Johnny could improve his game. I'm not sure Ed had noticed Johnny was essentially playing with one hand. On our twelfth hole Johnny hit his best drive of the day. Ed was quick to point out Johnny had finally made the swing move Ed was telling him to do and that is what produced Johnny's terrific shot. I couldn't take it anymore. As we were walking down the fairway I asked Johnny how he was handling Ed with such grace and his response was awesome and something I will never forget. Johnny was in agreement that Ed could be a little annoying, but Johnny was playing golf with Ed for 5 hours and then leaving it on the course. Ed was playing 5 hours of golf with Johnny U. And if Ed was getting a lifetime worth of stories about him giving Johnny U lessons on the course then why not give him that pleasure? WOW!

What a great lesson of patience and grace! From that day on I vowed to try and never get upset or annoyed. Johnny was able to see that Ed was just excited. And, Johnny could choose to be aggravated or to still be happy and enjoy himself. To me that was the ultimate example of choosing one's disposition because you can. You can't always choose your situation. It is so much easier to be easy going and to let things be "water off a ducks back". It takes a lot of energy and effort to be upset and mad. And, those negative emotions do absolutely nothing for you. I can speak from experience they definitely don't do anything for you on the golf course!

Jill McGill

From: **Jim McLean**

1994 PGA National Teacher of the
Year, owner of Jim McLean Golf
Schools

Nicholas,

Through playing the game of golf I have learned many things
myself, and then through teaching the game of golf I believe I
have learned even more. For one thing, the more I have studied
the golf swing the more I realize there are many ways to be
successful. I sometimes feel the more I study, the less I know!
there is always something in the golf swing that can surprise even
the most dedicated instructor.

So one piece of advice is to be yourself. Be an individual. Of
course this applies to all things, even beyond golf. For sure we
will learn from our teachers, and we will learn from watching
experts in things we want to improve, but it has been my
observation that the greatest people do things "their own special
way". Remember that a copy is never quite as good as the
original. So listen to others and watch the best, but always keep
some of your own technique, and most importantly believe in
yourself.

Nothing is more important than "self believe" and "the desire"
to do something special. Those two things will carry you a long
way in golf, or in any other endeavor you attempt. Do it with
all your heart and be the best you can be. That is total success in
my book.

Golf is one game you can play your entire life, and you can play it at any level with great enjoyment. An average week-end golfer can play with a Tiger Woods and have a competitive game. You can play the same golf course, and both you and Tiger Woods could get equal enjoyment from that round of golf. I do not believe there is any other sport where this could happen.

You will play with your Dad, and other members of your family for many years. You will go to great places, and have great times. Golf will teach you lot's of patience, as you will find that golf can not be defeated. You will find that golf is also a game of upgrading and constant adjustments...just like life. You will have to deal with bad shots, and bad days but you will learn how to do this. Golf teaches you so much about life. It's a game that get's into your blood and you will always have a kinship with anyone else, anywhere in the world, that plays this great game.

I wish you all the very best.
Jim McLean

From: **Steve Melnyk**

American professional golfer and
golf sportscaster, won both the U.S.
Amateur and British Amateur

Dear Nick,

1. Make a difference – to yourself, your family, your friends. Don't accept that you CAN'T do it. Persevere and be persistent.

2. Don't be afraid to fail – don't take the safe route, and know that it's OK to not be successful the first time. Like I used to tell my Little League players – it's OK to strike out, but DON'T strike out with the bat on your shoulder.

3. Be true to your faith – it will forever guide you, help shape your values, help you understand how to treat others, and most of all provide a moral compass always.

Steve Melnyk

From: **Eddie Merrins**

Golf Professional Emeritus, Bel-Air
Country Club

Dear Nick,

Golf is a game of problem solving. For every shot there is a
positive solution. Like in life, our decisions must be prudent.
Doubt, fear and regret come from being tentative or negative.

Swing the Handle!

Eddie Merrins

From: **Phil Mickelson**

American professional golfer, won
42 events on the PGA Tour, World
Golf Hall of Fame Member

Dear Nick:

The most important thing in life is your family. They are the people who care about you + will always be there for you. Success in life has nothing to do with possessions. It has everything to do with improving the quality of life for those around you. making other peoples' lives more enjoyable will make you feel like, and be, a success.

Sincerely,

P.S. Enjoy your life and good luck.

From: **Steve Mona**

World Golf Foundation's chief
executive officer since 2008

Dear Nick,

Here is my advice to you, based on 50 years of living life and 38
years of playing golf:

1. Always tell the truth – on your scorecard, in conversations
   and in what you write. While it may be uncomfortable to
   do so at times, you will never have to worry about what you
   told someone.

2. Always take the high road. While it may be tempting to
   get down in the dirt and sling a little mud, or to gossip
   when someone else is not present, you wind up the lesser
   person for having done so.

3. Always honor your commitments. If you say you're
   going to do something, do it by the time you said you
   would. If you can't, then say so and say when you are
   going to get it done. If you do this as a matter of habit,
   you'll be ahead of about 90 per cent of the people you'll
   encounter in life.

4. When you're talking with someone, make that person the
   only person in the world for that period of time. You'll
   be amazed at how few people look someone in the eye

and actively listen to what they are saying when having a conversation. Do it and you'll be in the upper ten percent, guaranteed.

5. People would rather play with a poor golfer with good manners, a positive attitude and who plays quickly than an excellent golfer with bad manners, a poor attitude and who plays slowly. Every time.

6. Remember that the caddies, beverage cart drivers, locker room attendants, people who pick up your bag when you arrive at the golf course, clean your clubs when you're finished with a round and put your clubs back in your car when it's time to leave are depending on your tip to make a living. None of them is getting rich, but they may be paying for their college education with that job. Tip them accordingly.

7. Never get behind the steering wheel of a car after you've had "a few." If you're with someone who hasn't, ask them to take you home. If you aren't, call a taxi, or a family member or a friend to pick you up. Too many people have lost their lives or ruined their or other persons' lives by driving a vehicle when they shouldn't have.

8. Smile. It doesn't cost anything and it makes those around you feel better about you and themselves. You should also surround yourself with people who smile often – they will pick you up and will rarely, if ever, drag you down.

I hope that you live in interesting times and that you are put in a position where you can make a positive impact on society, a family, or a single person. Because, when it's all over, that's what matters most.

Sincerely,
Steve Mona

From: **T.P. Mulrooney**
Stand-up golf comedian

Dear Nick,

Do you like Harry Potter and Star Wars, as does my 8-year-old son, Desmond? If you do, you have a better understanding of those great stories than other people. Why? Because you're a golfer. Sure, Harry has his magic wand and Anakin has his light saber. But you've got your 5-iron. All three are just sticks. But after a lot of practice and discipline, they become powerful tools for their masters.

But the most powerful are those who master themselves as well. Golf tests you, Nick. It demands you not only discipline yourself, but PENALIZE yourself. That takes character, the same weightless, invisible stuff it takes to perform well under pressure. The more you practice good character the more powerful it gets.

Harry overcame the evil Lord Voldemort because he wouldn't turn to evil even when his life was on the line. As for Anakin, he gave in to evil, The Dark Side. He became Darth Vader and wore a black helmet and mask the rest of his life. Maybe he was ashamed of himself.

Great golfers like Tiger Woods and Arnold Palmer are proud of themselves, probably because they're not just great golfers---they have great character. And if you notice....they seem to smile a lot. Hmmm. Maybe there's something to this character stuff.

Your Friend,
T.P. Mulrooney
a.k.a. The Golf Comic

From: **Jim Nantz**

American sportscaster and former
University of Houston golfer

Dear Nick,

1. Do everything with integrity.

2. Give everyone your respect and their dignitiy.

3. Count your blessings!

With warm wishes,
Jim Nantz

From: **Leroy Neiman**

American artist, known for his
expressionit paintings of athletes,
musicians and sporting events

Dear Nick,

As Duke Ellington once told me, "Life is the process of
becoming more of what we already are" so shape up early!

LeRoy Nemian
March 14, 2006

Dear Nicholas,

Your father asked me to answer a question to help you be a success in life. He obviously loves you a great deal, so you're blessed to have such a father. My advice would be for you to love and honor both your parents always, as the Bible promises if you do, you'll do well and have a long life. And also, you need to seek God, study his Word, and try hard to become as much like Christ as you can be.

Sincerely,

Byron Nelson

POSTMARK

From: **Rick Newell**

Creator of "Life in the Trap" cartoons and comics

DEAR NICK,

IT HAS BEEN SAID...
WATCH YOUR THOUGHTS; THEY BECOME WORDS.
WATCH YOUR WORDS; THEY BECOME ACTION.
WATCH YOUR ACTIONS; THEY BECOME HABITS.
WATCH YOUR HABITS; THEY BECOME CHARACTER.
WATCH YOUR CHARACTER; IT BECOMES YOUR DESTINY.
                    (AUTHOR UNKNOWN)

GOLF AND LIFE SHARE THE ATTRIBUTE THAT SMALL AMOUNTS OF SEEMINGLY INSIGNIFICANT THOUGHTS, WORDS, ACTIONS AND HABITS CAN AMOUNT TO A GREAT DEAL OVER TIME. ASK ANY GREAT GOLFER AND THEY WILL TELL YOU THAT THE HOURS SPENT PRACTICING THE PROPER SWING HELPED FORM THE HABITS THAT NATURALLY EXPRESS THEMSELVES ON THE GOLF COURSE. SMALL AMOUNTS OF LEARNING OVER A LONG PERIOD OF TIME CREATE A VAST RESERVE THAT CAN BE CALLED UPON IN THE STICKIEST OF SITUATIONS ON THE GOLF COURSE.

SIMILARLY, AS THE QUOTE ABOVE SUGGESTS, THE SEEMINGLY INSIGNIFICANT THINGS IN LIFE CAN ADD UP TO A GREAT DESTINY. WHAT DO YOU THINK ABOUT DURING THE VAST STRETCHES OF YOUR DAY? HOW DO YOU SPEND YOUR FREE TIME? DOES IT REFINE YOU? WHAT YOU CHOOSE READ, WATCH AND DO SHAPES WHAT YOU THINK ABOUT. WHAT YOU THINK ABOUT IS THE DOORWAY TO WHO YOU WILL BECOME.

GOLF AND LIFE ARE SIMILAR IN MANY RESPECTS, BUT THEY DIFFER IN ONE IMPORTANT WAY. ONE OR TWO BAD SWINGS DO NOT RUIN A GREAT GOLFER. IN LIFE, HOWEVER, ONE OR TWO BAD CHOICES CAN DESTROY A PERSON'S CHARACTER AND DESTINY FOREVER. THAT IS WHY IT IS DOUBLY IMPORTANT TO BE VIGILANT AND DEDICATED TO WHAT OCCUPIES OUR MINDS.

SO, NICK, WATCH YOUR THOUGHTS, WORDS, ACTIONS, HABITS AND CHARACTER. THEY WILL BE WHAT YOU ARE REMEMBERED FOR YOU... BOTH ON AND OFF THE COURSE.

YOUR FRIENDS,

DUFF AND CLAY FROM 'LIFE IN THE TRAP'.

WATCHING THE BALL HELPS TOO.

From: **Jack Nicklaus**

American professional golfer, winner
of 18 career major championships,
World Golf Hall of Fame Member

Dear Nick,

I think growing up is a lot harder for children today than it
was when I was your age. You face more difficult choices and
experience greater pressures than earlier generations. But I hope
you will accept that challenge gratefully, because you live in a
country of tremendous opportunities and prosperity. May you
find what you love in life, work hard to achieve your dreams,
appreciate the people who help you along the way, and always
strive to love your life with integrity, fairness and respect for
others.

Best wishes,
Jack Nicklaus
June 8, 2004

From: **Greg Norman**

Australian professional golfer and
enterpreneur, winner of 1986 and
1993 British Open

Dear Nick,

These are bits of advice and pearls of wisdom that I can offer you
from my experience as a Professional Golfer and in my personal
life:

The way to be a success in life is to make a decision using good
judgement and never look back.

The most important thing in the world are family and friends.

Love is the unconditional devotion to someone.

And happiness is doing the things you love to do!

Best wishes for a very healthy, happy and successful life!

Yours sincerely,
Greg Norman
September 19, 2001

From: **Michael O'Keefe**

American film and television actor, lead actor in *Caddyshack* as Danny Noonan

Dear Nicholas,

Your dad sounds like an interesting guy. Getting successful people to write you a few inspiring words is a novel idea so I am going to give it a whack.

I always liked what Joseph Campbell said about it:

"Follow your bliss."

So much of what we do in our lives can appear mundane and that can lead to disinterest. Find something that creates a passion in you to get what your after, whatever that is. If you can, be of service to your community while you pursue your dreams. The most satisfying experiences I've ever had were in giving something back to the world.

Be yourself. If you don't who will?

Later,
Michael O'Keefe
September 4, 2003

From: **Mark O'Meara**

American professional golfer and
World Golf Hall of Fame Member

Dear Nick,

In life it is always best to take the high road. Treat people with respect, have good manners and smile. These characteristics will help you tremendously in your life. Remember you are either getting better or worst! Choose to get <u>better</u>!!

All My Best!
Mark O'Meara

From: **Lorena Ochoa**

Mexican professional golfer, top-ranked female golfer in the world for more than three years

Dear Nick,

A lesson from golf...

All I've learned and all the things I did on the golf course influenced me and helped me to be the person I am right now. I think the golf course is the best way to learn, to grow. It helps you make decisions, recover from the bad times, from errors and problems, control the pressure, and to control the mind, especially when you are nervous. So all you learn on a golf course is really important and helps you apply it to your daily life.

The best experiences on the golf course...

What I liked and enjoyed most is to play golf with my family and friends. When I was a little girl I used to play on a golf course in Mexico. I loved being with my friends and playing together. Later on when I became a Pro, I will never forget the first time I played with Annika Sorenstam. At that time, she was the number one player in the world and I really enjoyed that moment. I will never forget the impression I had to see her, to play with her and to walk in the fairway with her. I always thought I wanted to be like her in the future and become the number one player in the world. It helped me a lot, inspiring me and motivating me.

An advice to succeed in golf…

Well, I think the most important thing for young golfers is practicing golf because they enjoy it, have a good time, and like to spend hours a day practicing. To become a professional golfer, I always recommend following the advice of the coaches. Correct the problems on the swing so in the future they can have a solid one.

5 simple recommendations…

Always be on time for classes or a tournament. It gives a very bad impression if you are late. The rush does not help you to play well. Take your time.

Bring food in the golf bag. I always take a banana between holes 6 or 7, and a half of a sandwich between holes 12 or 13 to be well nourished because of the long hours on the golf course.

Sun block is very important.

Keep your golf bag and clubs very clean. I like to check all my equipment the night before a tournament. Be sure everything is in perfect condition, and have enough golf balls to play.

A cap helps protect your from the sun and keeps your hair out of your face. It can also be used as lucky. When I was little, I had my lucky hats and I liked to change the caps depending on the day that I played. You feel confident with a cap that you like or you have affection for.

Lorena Ochoa

From: **Jesse Ortiz**

Golf club designer

Dear Nick,

I am much honored to have been asked by your Dad to write a few words of wisdom for you. I think that your Dad is giving you a tremendous gift for life. I hope that you will use some of the letters to best chart your path through life.

Nick, choose a vocation that you enjoy. If you have passion for what you do, it won't feel like work. Expertise, devotion and success will come. Don't take any shortcuts to being the best at what you do. Cutting corners will never earn you the respect you desire and deserve. If you love what you do, it will be easy to stay focused on becoming the best. That doesn't mean success will come easy, because none of the good things in life come easy. Being focused means, believing in yourself so strongly that you commit yourself to being the best. The inevitable criticisms, disappointments, and failures are only temporary setbacks in your quest to success and happiness.

Always remember that you cannot attain you goals by yourself. You will need help and those who support you should never be forgotten; particularly your family. There will be time when you will have doubts, but know that they will love you unconditionally. Stay humble; be kind and appreciative to those who encourage you early on. The world does not owe you anything, so never take good fortune for granted. You are already a very fortunate young man to have a father who is paving the road and filling the potholes of life with his collections of wisdom. Use this gift wisely…I'm pulling for you!

My Warmest Regards,
Jesse Ortiz

From: **Arnold Palmer**

American professional golfer

Dear Nick:

If I may offer you some advice, I think you will find life more enjoyable and fulfilling by embracing some of the following tenets:

- Treat others as you would want to be treated.
- Courtesy and respect are important principles of good manners to follow.
- Don't brag to people about how good you are at something. Show them.
- Win but do it by following the rules.
- Knowing when to speak is just as important as knowing what to say.
- Never underestimate the importance of a good education.

Sincerely,

Arnold Palmer

From: **Dr. Joseph Parent**

PGA Tour instructor, corporate speaker, Top Ten Mental Game coach, author of *Zen Golf*

Dear Nick,

I'm glad your Dad asked me to write to you about success, as it offers the opportunity to examine my own journey – reflecting on the past, taking inventory of the present, and looking to the future.

Here are some thoughts that you may find helpful for envisioning, working toward, and measuring your success in golf and in life:

True success is an authentic, self-aware, fully actualized state of being. It is not merely a checklist of achievements, measured by wealth or fame. It is an application of intention and effort in a meaningful endeavor. Success is a process, not an address.

Success is very much like a golf swing – neither one is really a thing, but people talk about them that way. Since you are always changing and growing, neither your swing nor your success can be a static thing - they must also grow and evolve.

Successful action involves a willingness to take risks. If you don't put yourself in a position where there is a chance of failure, you'll never be in a position where you have a chance of success. Like a turtle, if you don't stick your neck out, you never get anywhere.

Success takes time – it doesn't happen instantly. I am often asked how long it took to write it my first book, *Zen Golf*, which is regarded as a great success. While the actual composition and editing took just a few months, my answer is, "twenty years." The lessons conveyed in the book took at least twenty years to learn, experience and integrate into my life in a way that I could then communicate them authentically to others.

Will the measure of your success be the number of victories or possessions you accumulate, or the way you impact peoples' lives? Jack Nicklaus will be remembered as much for his character and sportsmanship as for his major championships. The measure of success is more about what you can give than what you can get.

True success is not the total of what you did or what you have. It is the manifestation of your qualities as a person, as well as the quality of the person you are continually becoming. It is not about looking back to see what you've done, but the extent to which you have the confidence to continually look forward with no hesitation and strive to become the best person you can be.

I hope these thoughts will help you to enjoy your journey toward true success.

Fairways and Greens,
Dr. Joe Parent

From: **Jerry Pate**

American professional golfer, winner
of 1976 U.S. Open

Dear Nick,

A few of the lessons I learned in life from my father were based
on his sayings and are ones I tried to love my life by.

The more your practice, the luckier you get.

Luck has an affinity to follow skill.

Expect what you inspect.

Tomorrow never comes.

If you lie down with dogs, you get fleas.

You can't stay up with the night owls and soar with the eagles.

It's better to be thought a fool than to speak and leave no doubt.

Live today as if it were your last.

Some of the most inspiring words of wisdom I have been given
since returning to the Champions Tour are from Isaiah 40:29-
31, "He strengthens those who are weak and tired. Even those
who are young grow weak. Young people can fall exhausted. But
those who trust in the Lord will find their strength renewed.

They will rise on wings like eagles. They will run and not get weary. They will walk and not grow weak."

Jerry Pate

From: **Suzann Pettersen**

Norwegian professional golfer, plays
mainly on the U.S.-based LPGA
Tour

Dear Nick,

My Best Advice:

To be patient and trust your own skills and ability.

Appreciate what you have and never be afraid to fail, but to learn
from life and make the best out of it.

Suzann Pettersen

From: **Gary Player**

South African professional golfer
with 165 professional wins and
World Golf Hall of Fame Member

Dear Nick,

The ability to accept adversity and overcome it is one of the most
important virtues because it offers us the greatest opportunities
for growth.

Sincerely,
Gary Player
2007

From: **Nick Price**

Zimbabwean professional golfer, won three major championships in his career, World Golf Hall of Fame Member

Dear Nick,

For me, the most important characteristic any person can have, is always wanting to get better and improve oneself. For some people, that progress is slow, but steady as it was for me. Each year, I tried to make my golf game more complete and better than the year before. Being your own critic is also very important. Knowing where and how to get better has to come from you.

There will always be people who have more talent than you. However, practice and perseverance will always outlast talent.

Sincerely,
Nick Price
August 20, 2014

From: **Harold Ramis**

American actor, director and writer
specializing in comedy, including
Caddyshack

Dear Nick,

Always remember that character is destiny. So be good and be
happy. And remember this too:

"The miracle is not to walk on water; the miracle is to walk on
the green earth, dwelling deeply in the present moment and
feeling truly alive."

Love, luck and all good things,
Harold Ramis

From: **Anna Rawson**

Australian professional golfer and model

Dear Nicky,

Always know that you control your own destiny. You and ONLY you control the actions of your life. You have a choice to make your life exceptional, mediocre or terrible. No one else decides this or you; it's completely up to you. To make your life exceptional allow yourself to DREAM BIG! Whatever I have dreamed for in my life, I have achieved. I don't know why this is, but I know that if you do the same you will achieve your dreams, or at least come very close. Anything is possible, if you believe it!

Anna Rawson

From: **Beatriz Recari**

Spanish professional golfer on the
U.S.-based LPGA Tour and the
Ladies European Tour

Dear Nick:

Play for The love of The game.
Play to always challenge yourself
to get better. Strive for excellence.
Play because you love it.
Enjoy The challenge!
Believe in yourself always!

Beatriz Recari

From: **Katherine Roberts**

Founder of Yoga for Golfers

Dear Nicholas,

Golf teaches us so many lessons. The obvious ones; enjoy your friends, appreciate the outdoors, get some exercise and have fun. The less obvious - the ethics of conducting ourselves and treating others with respect, the value of honesty and hard work. The even more subtle lessons are how to live with the results of each shot there for how to live in acceptance, learning to be present, quieting and focusing the mind, visualizing what you want to create.

A friend of mine conducted a study on "the joy of the game". He sat off the eighteenth green for two weeks and asked every golfer, "How was your round?" The younger golfers shared their unbridled joy for the game, the camaraderie, shared experiences of "crushing the ball" so far they hit it into the water, or sinking a long putt and getting to do the Tiger "pump". The older golfers had a more negative and self-critical response, typically having to do with their score, complaining about something that went wrong in the round.

We often look to our elders for guidance because of their valuable experience. I have been asked to impart to you wisdom from the game of golf but the reality is you have so much to teach us. If golfers approached the game with the boundless joy of a young man, the curiosity of a child, we would be better golfers.

Katherine Roberts

From: **Chi Chi Rodriguez**

Puerto Rican professional golfer, inducted in the World Golf Hall of Fame

Dear Nicholas,

A poor man does not have anything to prove. A rich man has to prove himself all the time! You need to prove you are worthy of what you accomplish. Remembering the hard times of your childhood does that. For me, I always knew that what other people had – material things – I could eventually get. And what I had – hunger and desire born of true hardship – they could never get! I don't think of being poor as a disadvantage; I though it was lucky because it made me a stronger person.

I would rather live rich and die poor; than die rich and live poor. Remember, you have to give. Takers eat well, givers sleep well. I get into bed, close my eyes, and I am out. When you enjoy life, share with others and have peace of mind, you have everything. I was a mental millionaire long before my bank account caught up.

When money, wisdom, and compassion are used as tools instead of weapons, wonderful things can be built and lives can be changed.

Remember that when you die, what you take with you is what you leave behind!

I truly believe that there are no bad kids, only society and people make them bad. You and your friends will be out next Senators, Congressmen, CEO's, possibly even the President of the United States – make us proud!

God Bless you,
Juan "Chi Chi" Rodriguez

From: **Doug Sanders**

Professional golfer

Dear Nick,

A winner makes a commitment and a Loser makes a promise. Set goals that's hard to reach but are reachable but, once you reach them set new goals because you always have to have a goal to look forward to, to be successful. When you make a mistake first tell people, I am sorry I made a mistake, that makes you a winner. But, when you make excuses you're a loser. Every night look in the mirror at yourself and say "I like you". If you can, then you are a true winner.

If you play Golf, Just swing "slow and easy".

Doug Sanders

From: **Peter Thomson**

World Golf Hall of Fame member,
the Australian golfer is a 5-time The
Open Championship winner

Dear Nick,

I thought what sort of thing you might like from me. The
following came to mind. It is a letter my son wrote to a friend
at Royal Melbourne recently, and was published in the Club
Newsletter. It epitomizes my attitude to young golfers. I hope
you might find it amusing!

Dear Paul,

*I had a delightful game yesterday with my father,
and two other members of the club.*

*As you probably know, my father has always been
very reticent about giving playing tips to anyone,
(family included), on the dubious grounds that
golf is too simple a game for much advice giving.
I have spent years trying to extract advice from
him but to little avail. His replies to questions
about technique have always been obscure, but
yesterday I think he reached a new height. On
the first tee I suggested to him that a firmer grip
on the shaft with the little finger of the upper
hand ought to result in a more reliable shot. He
considered this theory for some moments and then*

replied, "Try anything".

Kind regards,
Andrew.

My best wishes.
Peter Thomson

Dear Nick,

Hi, my name is Alexi Thompson ("Lexi"). I am just 15 years old and will be turning pro in one month. I will be a professional golfer which is my passion in life. I love playing golf.

The best lesson I have learned in my life is to follow your dreams and the things you love to do. Life is precious and you should live it to the fullest.

One other lesson is to love your family and friends because they are your support and backbone in you life. We can learn great long term lesson from them that will carry us through our journey.

Love,
Lexi

Hopefully you will be on of my biggest fans one day.

From: **Carol Semple Thompson**

American golfer, World Golf Hall of Fame Member

Dear Nick,

You are a lucky young man to have a father so interested in the game of golf. It is the most challenging interesting and fun game you will ever experience. It can take you all over the world to strange and exotic places and introduce you to interesting and accomplished people. It is a game for all ages, one you can play your whole life.

My introduction to golf came through my parents, both scratch players addicted to the game. My father mandated that all five of us children learn to play well enough to break 90, then we were allowed to quit. My siblings did quite, but they have all come back to play with their own children. I was the one who fell in love with golf and the competition it provided.

I have found that a round of golf invariably tests me both mentally and physically. Typically I experience a whole range of emotions in 18 holes – frustration, elation, depression, excitement, satisfaction. If you learn to control your emotions on the golf course you will be well equipped for life.

So enjoy your introduction to golf and appreciate all your time together with your father. My father is gone now, but I still have a wonderful time playing with my 86-year-old mother. Golf challenges both of us each and every day.

Wishing you all the best,
Carol Semple Thompson

From: **Patty Sheehan**

American professional golfer, won six major championships and 35 LGPA Tour events, World Hall of Fame Member

Dear Nick,

Let me first say what a privilege it is to be able to write to you at such a young age! Thank you!!

First let me stress how important <u>honesty</u> is. Always tell the truth no matter what.

Second, being able to say <u>I'm sorry</u> and mean it, is a wonderful way to treat people fairly.

Third, <u>determination</u> will carry you further than you think you can go.

Fourth, <u>consideration</u> of others feelings.

Finally, <u>Love</u> – the greatest power of all.

Take pride in yourself Nick!

Love,
Patty Sheehan
April 19, 2014

From: **Marilynn Smith**

American former professional golfer, one of the thirteen founders of the LPGA in 1950, World Golf Hall of Fame Member

Dear Nick,

You Father has asked me to write his young man regarding some principles which I feel are important in life.

Do your best! Try to do your <u>best</u> in everything you do; whether it is trying to sink a three-foot putt or trying to figure our a math problem (Remember, Einstein failed math). Math and Science teach us how to think – think "Math is Beautiful"! Do your best and you will be happy. You cannot fail. You can accomplish almost everything you want if you are willing to work at it. ENJOY!

Honesty! Do not cheat on tests or on the golf course. It's OK to make mistakes; we all do, so own up to them and try not to make the same mistake again. One does not have to win a tournament to be a WINNER in life.

Be Happy! No one wants to be around a 'grump'. Be gracious in winning or losing on the golf course, just as you would be gracious if you win or lose a Spelling Bee competition.

Patience! Have patience with yourself as well as with others. If someone doesn't learn as fast as you, you have patient with them.

Parents! Feel comfortable in telling your parents how you feel about golf. Some youngsters don't want to be pushed into playing golf, or playing as well as their parents want them to play. Kids are people too and have a right to express themselves. Help you parents understand your feelings.

Find something that is special to you! Each of us can make a difference and contribute to society.

Golden Rule! My Father told me as a youngster to follow the <u>Golden Rule</u>.

Remember to always be the best person you can be! Be thankful for what you have – Family, Friends, God and Teachers.

Nick, you are one lucky fella to have the parents you have. God bless you and your Mother and Father.

Warm regards,
Marilynn Smith
February 21, 2008

From: **Sam Snead**

American professional golfer, winner
of 82 PGA Tour events, World Golf
Hall of Fame Member

Dear Nick,

Proclaim Jesus Christ as your Lord and Savior and serve him
with your life. Get the best education that you can acquire at
Mom & Dad's expense. Use your education to serve others and
to find fulfillment in life. Choose your wife wisely and carefully
and then stick it out no matter how tough or hard it gets (stay
married). Find Joy, Peace and Humor in everyday life and then
share it with those around you. Always give more than you get.
Under promise—over deliver. Hold you family Near & Dear.
Don't take them for granted.

Best Wishes,
Sam Snead

From: **Joseph Steranka**

Chief Global Strategist of Buffalo
Communications, former PGA of
America CEO

Dear Nick,

When I was young, I played golf with a sense of wonderment
and joy. How could you swing so easy and make such a little ball
go so far. Just a fun game with a stick and a ball.

The courses of my youth were simple and straightforward…
short, straight holes, few bunkers or hazards and greens with
little speed of movement. Hit it straight and the ball goes in the
hole.

As life progressed, so too did my experience with golf. My PGA
Professionals taught me about the "feel" of shots and the strategy
of playing a hole. I needed it because the courses I was now
playing were much more challenging. They had rough. They had
frightening waters hazards. They had deep bunkers. They had
fast and undulating greens.

The greater the challenge of the course, the more I appreciated
the wisdom of my pro. And, I appreciated and enjoyed the
success of playing a tough hole or course, and coming out on
top. I still do.

Nicholas, as you grow up, I believe you will see how much
golf is like life itself…simple and carefree at the start and more

challenging as you learn new things. There are two things that will remain the same along the way…you will always relish the challenge and success and there will always be someone to help you.

And, if you find you really love the game, you can become one of those people who helps others; a PGA Professional.

Fairways and greens,
Joseph P. Steranka
June 25, 2008

From: **Louise Suggs**

American professional golfer, one of
the founders of the LPGA Tour

Dear Nick,

Knock the "Hell" out of the golf ball—it'll come down
somewhere.

Louise Suggs

From: **Perry Swenson**

American professional golfer, played on the Futures Tour and in LPGA events

Dear Nick,

I once heard someone say, "the game of golf is the ultimate test of integrity in action." The small lessons that I have learned growing up playing the game of golf, translate directly into the game of life. It's playing the ball as it lies instead of taking a mulligan, and taking the penalty when no one is watching!

One lesson I learned at a very young age was how easy it is to cheat while golfing. We've heard the saying, "Golf reveals character" and golf also builds character. The dictionary defines character as the moral qualities and ethical standards that make up the inner nature of a person. The conviction to not cheat and to play honestly comes from the determination to choose to do your best and not let the temptation to "enhance" our score by dishonestly lowering it.

At a very young age, I chose to be honest. I liked the free feeling of guilt-free living. I knew I had to be true to myself. Honesty allows us not to have to live with the feeling of condemnation deep in our souls. I may have lost a round of golf or the match, but I can still "look at myself in the mirror" and know that I was honest. This gives my spirit freedom, for I know I will win some and lose some. My parents have always told me that "my best is good enough!" If I have done my best and still scored below my expectations, I can hold my head up high because I stayed true to myself.

I will never forget this poem I ran across during my junior year at the University of Texas. I played on the women's golf team and we really had four great years! I still remember reading this poem out loud to my roommate, Katie, who played on the women's tennis team. It's called, "The Man in the Mirror."

"When you get what you want in your struggle for self,
And the world make you king for a day,
Then go to the mirror and look at yourself
And see what the man has to say

For it isn't man's father, mother or wife
Whose judgment upon him must pass
The fellows whose verdict counts most in his life
Is the man staring back from the glass

He's the fellow to please, never mind all the rest
For he's with you clear up to the end
And you've passed your most dangerous, difficult test
If the man in the glass is your friend

You can fool the whole world down the pathway of years
And get pats on the back as you pass
But your final reward will be heartache and tears
If you've cheated the Man in the glass!"

I look forward to seeing where this wonderful game of golf takes us! I also look forward to continuing to play the "ball as it lies" in both golf and my life.

Always,
Perry Swenson
March 29, 2008

From: **Frank "Sandy" Tatum, Jr.**

Former amateur golfer, 1942 NCAA
Champion, former USGA President

Dear Nicholas,

It may be stretching it a bit to call it wisdom, but I do have some thoughts about opportunities a young golfer has to enrich his or her life.

Make sure that you are doing everything you can to be the best golfer you can be. A fundamental part of that process is to develop understanding, and appreciation for the values a golfer needs to develop.

Those values include:

1. Understanding the rules and consistently playing in accord with them;

2. Appropriate etiquette so that the experience of those with whom you play is enhanced;

3. Accepting the challenges posed in playing the game and doing your best to deal with them in good grace and humor;

4. Setting realistic golas for how well you can play, adjusting them as your improve; and

5. Being always grateful for having golf in your life.

Each element of foregoing advice applies to how you develop your life so that you can be the most effective person you can be.

Both in regard to your golf game and your life, adopt the mantra GO FOR IT!

Sandy Tatum
September 14, 2007

From: **Frank Thomas**

Former technical director of the USGA, golf inventor of the graphite shaft

Dear Nick,

Man is peculiar in that we seek to rid ourselves of all obstacles while at the same time we assemble a set of artificial difficulties and call this a game. Golf is one of only a few activities, which allows us to satisfy a subconscious urge to evaluate ourselves but one can only get an accurate measure if we are true to ourselves. Whatever challenge you face in life, it is vital to do your best to cope with it and never give up. For this, you will be self fulfilled and a better person.

Frank Thomas

From: **Kelly Tighlman**

Boradcaster for The Golf Channel,
PGA Tour's first female lead golf
announcer

Dear Nick,

In all my years of being around the game of golf, I have learned
an important lesson. Golf, like life, is full of unexpected twists
and turns. It's one of the many reasons the game is so beautiful.
Just when you think you've sorted it out, your ball mysteriously
ends up in the rough again. While many become frustrated
when things don't go their way, I'm going to surprise you with
advice on how to handle it. I want you to get excited. That's
right, excited! This is an opportunity for you to really shine.

Many of Tiger Woods' greatest moments in major championship
history came after a substandard shot. In the final round of
the 2005 Masters, he sank that magical pitch shot on 16.
That wouldn't have happened if he hadn't missed the green on
his approach. Tiger once said the best shot of his remarkable
career was a 3 iron out of a fairway bunker in the 2002 PGA
Championship. Well, how did he get into that bunker? Do you
see where I'm going with this?

Golf has an unbelievable way of exposing your attitude and your
deepest fears. Do you shy away from your challenges or embrace
them? I encourage you to tackle them head on! When you're
practicing, prepare for any test the golf course can pose. When
the test finally comes, savor it and visualize a positive outcome.

These moments are what help you grow.

Congratulate yourself for the things that you did well and take a mental note of the things that went wrong so you can work on avoiding those mistakes in the future. Remember, success isn't only measured by score. A positive attitude will ultimately bring you happiness. Here's to hoping you always look forward to your next shot.

Your friend,
Kelly

From: **Bob Toski**

American golfer and teacher, 1954
PGA Tour leading money winner

Dear Nick,

Knowledge is power – used wisely, Principles are more important than preferences. Truth only hurts for the moment, but a lie hurts forever. Be honest with yourself and those you associate with.

Giving is receiving – but learned the hard way. Count your blessings every day.

All the best!
Bob Toski

From: **Lee Trevino**

American professional golfer, won six major championships over the course of his career, World Golf Hall of Fame Member

Dear Nick,

You will never go wrong if you tell your Mother and Father you love them every day.

And if you are ever a golfer, practice, practice. You'll be OK with a dad and mom like you have.

My best,
Lee Trevino

From: **Ty Tryon**

American professional golfer,
became at 17 years old the
youngest player to earn exempt
status via rqualifying school

Dear Nick,

Keep a smile on our face and your head down!

Best wishes in Life!
Ty Tryon

From: **Ken Venturi**

American professional golfer and
golf broadcaster, World Golf Hall of
Fame Member

Dear Nick,

You will never go wrong in life if every decision you make is
predicated on would my Mother and Father be proud of me.

All the best,
Ken Venturi

From: **Peter Ueberroth**

American executive, part owner of
Pebble Beach Company

Dear Nick:

Two things:

1. Be proud of your
   mother!
   Look out for her when
   she is older.

2. Ask questions — all your
   life — it is the best way
   to learn.

Pete Ueberroth

From: **Bob Vokey**

Mater Wedge designer, Titleist

Dear Nick,

Your Dad tells me you are interested in golf. Stick with it because it is a great game. Not only is it fun to play, but it teaches you many life lessons like honesty, trust and confidence in yourself. It also provides the opportunity to meet people from all walks of life with whom you would otherwise never cross paths.

Try and observe and absorb as much as you can from the people you meet and retain all that is good. Life is all about making decisions. Try to always make the correct one, but if you don't, learn from your mistakes and you will be successful.

Bob Vokey

From: **Robert von Hagge**

Golf course designer

Dear Nick,

You will be growing up in a much different society than I did. Everything today is happening at a very rapid pace compared to my formative years. I think things will be much more difficult for you to stay ahead of or even current with a lot of important and demanding "life" issues. Even with the spectacular technical advances we are experiencing, the requirements for today's society none-the-less keep bunching up ahead of one's ability to sort out and deal with.

Nick, my advice to you is to make it a habit to find quiet time and a comfortable way to retreat within yourself. Focus on the clear picture of "Nick" and achieving total success with the life goals you desire. I did, and still do it daily and it works. Don't hold back. Be specific in every detail in seeing yourself as you want to be and doing the things you want to do, successfully. Most times the desired results will occur in ways you did not foresee, however, they do seem to eventually somehow materialize.

There is no doubt that you live in the best country on earth. It is a miraculous place where you can do and be just about anything or anyone you desire and when your goals begin to take shape, you will feel deeply, the joy that comes with personal accomplishment.

For me, I still can't wait until the sun rises each day and that I may get another call from some different and perhaps exotic location in the world inquiring whether or not I would be interested in designing a beautiful golf course there.

Life is still a wonderful adventure!

Robert von Hagge
January 31, 2008

From: **Dennis Walters**

American professional golfer

Dear Nick,

My advice to you is when you are old enough give the game of golf a try. If it is for you, it is a wonderful lifetime recreation that teaches us valuable life lessons. Most of all though, golf is a lot of fun and therein lies my real bit of advice. Try to find something in life you really enjoy and are passionate about for you will do it to the best your ability. Striving for excellence is one of the many lessons golf teaches us. Always do your best and you will feel so much better. Wherever you may find your inspiration, I hope it leads you to a life of enjoyment and success!

Warmest regards,
Dennis Walters
November 12, 2007

From: **Lanny Wadkins**

American professional golfer, 1977
PGA Championship winner, World
Golf Hall of Fame Member

Dear Nick,

Live life as if there is no tomorrow! Treasure your friends and family – life is too short to have enemies. Set goals and work hard and dedicate yourself to achieving them. Smile a lot and remember true friends will be there for the good times and especially the bad.

All the Best,
Lanny Wadkins

From: **Tom Watson**

American professional golfer

Dear Nick:

Learn early in your life to say no...
and mean it.

Know yourself before passing judgement
on others.

Live every moment of your life as if
it might be your last.

And lastly always try to do the right
thing, even if no one is watching.

Best of luck.

Tom Watson

From: **D.A. Weibring**

American professional golfer, winner
of several tournaments including the
PGA Tour and Champions Tour

Dear Nick,

I was very fortunate growing up in a small town (Quincy, IL)
where life was not too complicated. The People were hard
working, friendly and very supportive. I was an only child with
parents who laid the foundation for my life.

My Parents taught me numerous values that I am very grateful
for today. They were always passionate about doing things the
right way, always looking to help others, and always respecting
their faith. If you go through life following these simple
principles along with treating others the way you wish to be
treated—I promise you a positive life!

Work hard—play hard and trust your faith!

All the Best
D.A. Weibring

From: **Tom Weiskopf**

American professional golfer and
course architect, played on the PGA
Tour and the Champions Tour, won
the 1973 British Open

Dear Nick,

It begins with knowing what you want to achieve in life. I
believe it is the attainment of personal goals to live the life you
imagined, not because of luck, but through cause and affect.
Through your first journey, alternative choices may become
available and lead to a completely different outcome for success.

Tom Weiskopf

From: **Michael Whan**

LPGA Commissioner

Dear Nick,

I would like to give you the same advice that my parents gave me. Both of these principles have guided me, and I hope they bring some comfort to you as well.

1. *Failure is a Dress Rehearsal for Success* – Don't be afraid to fail, but rather push yourself to be "willing" to fail on your way to dramatic improvement.

2. *Appreciation is Free, but its Value is Priceless* – As you progress in life, never forget to show real, genuine appreciation to those who take the time to help you with your journey. This goes way beyond family, so don't keep appreciation as a family-only gift.

Remember that simple phrases like "I'm sorry" and "thank you" will take you farther than you'll ever dream.

Michael Whan

From: **Jack Whitaker**

American sportscaster, worked for both CBS and ABC

Dear Nick,

Try to be honest with yourself and you will find a serenity that will allow you to realize your full potential as a human being.

And laugh a lot, especially at yourself -- and be as positive as possible -- The glass is always hall full not half empty. Remember, a 3 putt is better than a 4 putt --

All the best, Nick
Jack Whitaker

From: **Kathy Whitworth**

American professional golfer, World
Golf Hall of Fame Member

Dear Nick,

<u>Be Honest especially with yourself</u>.

<u>Never give up</u>!

Never be afraid to do the right <u>thing</u>.

All the best to you!
Kathy Whitworth

From: **Steve Williams**

MNZM, Caddyshack Racing and
caddy to Greg Norman, Raymond
Floyd, Tiger Woods and Adam
Scott

Dear Nick,

In golf it is widely accepted that you only get out what you put
in. To become a successful professional it take a tremendous
amount of dedication and commitment. In order to do this you
have to be prepared to make many sacrifices.

You could say the same about life that you only get out what you
put in. A person who is dedicated and passionate about life will
generally succeed in life.

I can honestly say from my experience as a professional caddy
that the game of golf is a great game to play and can only
enhance your life and make you a better person.

Sincerely,
Steve Williams

From: **Dr Gary Wiren**

PGA and World Golf Teachers Hall
of Fame Member

Dear Nick,

They say that golf is a game—but is more than that. It can be a
test—

Of your patience—

Of your temper—

Of your concentration and focus—

Of your practical intelligence—

Of your endurance—

Of your willingness to be mentored—

If you can pass these tests you will not only be a fine golfer, but a
success in life.

For more enjoyable and productive golf experiences
Gary Wiren
January 10, 2008

From: **Tiger Woods**

Winner of 14 Majors and 79
PGA Tour events, former NCAA
champion and career PGA Tour
money leader

Dear Nick,

Remember as you go through life that the greatest gift you will ever receive is the love of your parents. With the guidance and understanding from your parents, you will learn many valuable lessons. Lessons such as:

1. Respect your parents and elders

2. "Please" and "thank you" really are the magic words

3. Treat others as you would like to be treated

4. If you work hard, your dreams can come true

All the best to you, Nick, for a life filled with good health and happiness.

Yours sincerely,
Tiger Woods
October 1, 2002

Apprentice
House Press
Loyola University Maryland

Apprentice House is the country's only campus-based, student-staffed book publishing company. Directed by professors and industry professionals, it is a nonprofit activity of the Communication Department at Loyola University Maryland.

Using state-of-the-art technology and an experiential learning model of education, Apprentice House publishes books in untraditional ways. This dual responsibility as publishers and educators creates an unprecedented collaborative environment among faculty and students, while teaching tomorrow's editors, designers, and marketers.

Outside of class, progress on book projects is carried forth by the AH Book Publishing Club, a co-curricular campus organization supported by Loyola University Maryland's Office of Student Activities.

Eclectic and provocative, Apprentice House titles intend to entertain as well as spark dialogue on a variety of topics. Financial contributions to sustain the press's work are welcomed. Contributions are tax deductible to the fullest extent allowed by the IRS.

To learn more about Apprentice House books or to obtain submission guidelines, please visit www.apprenticehouse.com.

Apprentice House
Communication Department
Loyola University Maryland
4501 N. Charles Street
Baltimore, MD 21210
Ph: 410-617-5265 • Fax: 410-617-2198
info@apprenticehouse.com • www.apprenticehouse.com